The
Audacity
of
Truth

The
Audacity
of
Truth

A Bold Presentation of the
Issues Challenging our Country

Albert A. Hernandez, D. Div.

THE AUDACITY OF TRUTH
A BOLD PRESENTATION OF THE ISSUES CHALLENGING OUR COUNTRY

New King James Version (NKJV)
Scripture taken from the New King James Version®. Copyright © 1982 by Thomas Nelson. Used by permission. All rights reserved.

New International Version (NIV)
Holy Bible, New International Version®, NIV® Copyright ©1973, 1978, 1984, 2011 by Biblica, Inc.® Used by permission. All rights reserved worldwide.

iUniverse books may be ordered through booksellers or by contacting:

iUniverse
1663 Liberty Drive
Bloomington, IN 47403
www.iuniverse.com
1-800-Authors (1-800-288-4677)

ISBN: 978-1-5320-5871-4 (sc)
ISBN: 978-1-5320-5870-7 (e)

Library of Congress Control Number: 2018912206

Print information available on the last page.

iUniverse rev. date: 10/10/2018

Author's Note

S pelling and punctuation in some of the documents in this book have been modernized and certain graphic language used to convey the intended message. Ampersands have been converted. Footnotes have been omitted for the sake of brevity; a bibliography should suffice. Misspelled names have been reviewed and corrected for integrity. Abbreviations and acronyms are used only where applicable and necessary.

Truth will ultimately prevail where there is pains taken to bring it to light.

—George Washington

Contents

INTRODUCTION

The purpose of this book is not for self-glory or economic gain but rather for a unique presentation of the issues and problems facing our country—and what we *can do* about them. The subjects covered will vary. From health, politics, and war to religion and fiction, I will write about those things that impact society and our country as a whole. I will be brief and to the point. I will not bore you with status quo rhetoric and cumbersome statistics, for these are changing all the time and do not tell the whole story. Some of the material will be strong and bold; they will be *my* words, no one else's. What you are about to read is based on experience, knowledge, and intense study. I will pull no punches. Prepare yourself; this book is not for the meek or the weak. It is for the bold American who loves their country and wants to do something to save it. You are merely asked to absorb the information with an open mind and positive attitude. Whether you are Christian or not, Democrat or Republican, black or white, or whatever your status is, is not the point. It is the presentation of facts and a moral conviction that I wish to convey and share.

Why? Because our nation is under attack from all major fronts. From terrorist attacks to anti-patriotism, to religion, to our classrooms, we're in trouble. We are quickly losing our image as Americans. The American dream has become an American nightmare for many.

I hope and pray that this book will serve as a message of enlightenment and edification for the sake of righteousness and moral perspective. It is written in good faith and in the fear of the Lord. It is, in fact, a fervent and spiritual outcry for the salvation of our souls and our country. I will take you to places few dare to explore.

May God bless you and our United States of America.

We set our eyes not on what we see but on what we cannot see. What we see will last only a short time, but what we cannot see will last forever.

—2 Corinthians 4:18 NKJV

He who reads knows more. He who knows more has power. Knowledge is power.

—(aah)

CHAPTER 1

Why I Write

Why write a book? Don't I have anything better to do? Should I travel, go shopping, go to the movies, go out to a restaurant, and visit family or friends? Well, no, I don't have anything better to do. I've done all of the above. Traveling has become a hassle and is too expensive these days. Shopping makes no sense when you are retired and living on a limited income. Going to the movies is also expensive, and have you noticed the kind of movies they are making nowadays? Going out to eat is also getting costly, especially now with the economy.

The greatest peace and tranquility that I now enjoy is in my study, a solemn place that I have created for myself, when I need to be alone. It is there where I can write. It is there where I can actually feel my soul, where I can think, pray, and even cry when I have to. Every man should have a personal and private sanctuary. Even Jesus had His own private place. Now all this doesn't mean I don't enjoy life; of course I do. I count my blessings every day and thank God for what I have. But writing is a gift I've been blessed with. It took me years to realize this. My wife kept telling me I should write a book. So I am. I have some things to say to the nation and the world, things I know about.

Any man, if he is worth anything in life, should have the passion and desire to speak his mind. It was the pens of our founding fathers that formed this country with their writings of our Constitution. So when you see a letter or an article of mine, remember it's for a purpose and a reason. It's for a cause. For what good is all my knowledge and wisdom if I cannot share it with my fellow man? What good am I if I cannot speak my mind for the benefit of humankind? I am already dead if I don't.

I write mainly because I'm an American. I write because I'm free. I write because I care. I care about that soldier or marine on the front lines protecting our country. I care about that widow and the children who lost their father or mother to war. I care about the fathers and mothers who lost a son or a daughter. I care about that fellow vet in a VA hospital who is in constant pain and cannot move. I write because I care about that casket that arrives, covered with the American flag; it tears my heart apart every time I see it. I write because of the elderly and the poor that through no fault of their own have lost all they have. I write because of the sick who have been stricken with disease and are suffering. I write because of that precious innocent child that has been deprived of life due to cancer. I write because of those kids who lost their lives in those school shootings. I write because of the sick and suffering, so rampant in this country. And I write for that soul that does not believe in God, the one God will hold me accountable for if I don't bring him or her to salvation.

That's why I write.

This is what the Lord, the God of Israel says: "Write in a book
all the words I have spoken."
—Jeremiah 30:2 NKJV

The written word is what distinguishes us from animals.
—(aah)

CHAPTER 2

Is This America?

For all the nations have drunk of the wine of the wrath of her fornication, the kings of the earth have committed fornication with her, and the merchants of the earth have become rich through the abundance of her luxury … her plagues will come in one day—death and mourning and famine. And she will be utterly burned with fire, for strong is the Lord God who judges her … And the kings of the earth who committed fornication and lived luxuriously with her will weep and lament for her, when they see the smoke of her burning … for in one hour your judgment has come … And the merchants of the earth will weep and mourn over her, for no one buys their merchandise anymore … The Merchants of these things, who became rich by her, will stand at a distance for fear of her torment, weeping and wailing … For in one hour such great riches came to nothing.

—Revelation 19

We're in trouble, real trouble. Our country is changing drastically before our eyes. Our laws are practically worthless and unjust. Our health care is poor, with proposed cuts in Medicaid and Medicare. Veterans' benefits are also on the cutting board. Seniors are being denied care. The immigration problem is out of control. There is the threat of more war; a war with North Korea is imminent according to military experts. Russia remains a threat. China is also is taking us for a ride. And worst of all, Christianity is failing. The Muslim religion is the fastest-growing faith in our country as millions are converting to Allah. Did you know that?

We pledge allegiance, display our flags, sing the national anthem, and go through the motions of professed patriots. We do all those things claiming we are Americans. We say, "This is America, the greatest country on earth." But I wonder, is this really America? Is this the America I once knew? The America I went to war for? The America I love? There was a time when our country had at least a sense of decency, pride, and moral values. When marriage was between a man and a woman. When you didn't have to worry about getting shot or blown up by some terrorist. When cops were not ambushed, when politicians were more civil and not stupid and so arrogant. When our public schools taught us what we needed to learn and also how to behave; deportment was one of the areas that was graded in our early school years. Now they don't even show you how to write your name. When parents and teachers ruled, not spoiled and obnoxious brats. Now, a father or mother can go to jail if they spank their kids; forget that trip to the woodshed where your father would put the fear of parental discipline on your rear end—in other words, reminding you who was in charge. Those days are gone. But wait! Where's the father? He's been divorced. He's gone. Your mother now has to work two, maybe three, jobs to pay the bills and put food on the table. She's aging before your eyes, getting sicker every day. She's hurting. She's dying. I'm talking about the destruction of the American family. Is this America? I remember when we sat at the dinner table—Mom, Dad, and my brothers—enjoying a delicious meal and talking to each other. God, how I miss those days!

Having studied the scriptures for many years, since 1987, having served in the churches, having survived a war (Vietnam 1966–67), and observing what has happened to our country in the last several years, I've come to the chilling conclusion that the above scripture could very well depict the true character and fate of our nation and why we are experiencing such difficult times and so many tragedies.

At the writing of this book, there is chaos in our government and in our schools. We have a new and controversial president. The issues of the times are immigration, health care, war, terrorism, more war, and mass school shootings. The natural disasters, those huge hurricanes and fires, are devastating our land. Millions are losing their homes. More and more children are coming down with cancer. Scientists cannot explain this. Why is all this happening to us? Why is our country suffering so much? Frankly, I think God is trying to tell us something, to get our attention. Well, He has mine. The true man of God can see these things. He sees things others can't see. He's the prophet of the times, but the world will not listen to him. He will be shunned, ostracized, even persecuted.

But here is a cold fact: child pornography, the filth permeating the television airwaves, the homosexual and feminist movements that have forced legislation for the legalization of marriage between gays and lesbians, not to mention now the transgenders, the increase in abortions, the escalation of divorce, the rebellious and obnoxious youth, the mass killings and murders everywhere, and of course our dysfunctional national and local governments are signs that make us wonder if we are truly a nation under God anymore. It makes me wonder, Is God hearing our supplications? People are asking, How can all this happen and why? "God Bless America" is the outcry, but are His blessing really upon us?

Some would say this is just someone's opinion or philosophy. It's not. Return to the above scripture. It describes to a frightening degree the true character of our country's sin and impending doom. The words "poverty" and "terror" have become common terms to describe the status of our country. "Land of the free and home of the brave" is under fire. Our flag has been disgraced by Americans themselves. The rich get richer, the poor get poorer. From the highest office to the lowliest entity, greed and immorality reign. Even our laws are worthless, unjust. Our jails are swamped with victims of a corrupt system of government and laws. Men are killed by police officers because of race and color; in retaliation, policemen are ambushed. It's become a war within a war. Lawlessness abounds. Consider the following speech:

> So much of the time we are just lost. We say, please God, tell us what is right, what is true, where there is no justice.
>
> The rich win, the poor are powerless. We become tired of hearing people lie, and after a time, we become dead, we think of ourselves as victims, we become victims, we become … we become … weak. We doubt ourselves,

we doubt our beliefs. We doubt our institutions, and we doubt the law.

But today, you are the law. *You are the law.* Not some book, not the lawyers, not the marble statues or the trappings of the court. See, those are just symbols of our desire to be just. They are … they are, in fact, a prayer, a fervent and frightened prayer. In my religion, say act if ye had faith, faith will be given unto you. If we are to have faith in justice, we need only to believe in ourselves, and act in justice. See, I believe there is justice in our hearts.

This is from the movie *The Verdict,* with Paul Newman saying these words. This pretty much describes the sin of our nation. It is a truth we don't like to discuss or admit. But it's there.

No nation is above God no matter how rich and powerful it may be. No nation is exempt from His judgment. "Surely the nations are like a drop in a bucket; they are regarded as dust on the scales … before Him all nations are as nothing; they are regarded by Him as worthless and less than nothing" (Isaiah 40:15–17 NIV).

Whatever our beliefs are, whatever our religion or faith is, does not change the truth or the obvious. We are right now witnessing the end-times whether we want to realize it or not. The winds of war are already present, our governments are corrupt, our laws are useless, sickness and disease are rampant, and our planet is under attack. Doom and gloom jargon? No. Doom and gloom prophecy. But! There's hope in the Lord and only in the Lord. Consider the following:

"If my people who are called by My name will
humble themselves, and pray and
seek My face, and turn from their wicked ways, then I will hear from
heaven, and will forgive their sin and heal their land."
—2 Chronicles 7:14

Whatever our country stands for, that's who we are.
—(aah)

Health Care

A Brief Analysis of the Problem

I now want to discuss the problem of health care. It is my specialty. It was my profession. It is a problem that is affecting millions of Americans and one that is going to get worse. Therefore, this writing is for those who are concerned about their health before it deteriorates and for all those who work in the health care arena who are committed to the improvement of our American health care system.

Because the general contention is that health care is a right, and the lack of access to good health care for so many of our citizens is a moral outrage, it is imperative to recognize that no sector of this nation can any longer view its problems in isolation from the facts facing the delivery of health care. The health care dilemma is here now, and we have no choice but to face it. It will affect *every* American, sooner or later.

It is appalling that we are the only industrialized and civilized country in the world that does not actually *guarantee* at least basic health care for all our citizens. But American health care increasingly poses another powerful question: how will we ration care even for those who now get basic care as we increasingly face a system that will no longer be able to afford everything for everyone? A certain analytical prediction is that if the current rate of inflation for health care were to continue unchanged, in less than twenty years, health care would consume 100 percent of the gross national product ("Critical Issues in American Health Care—Doctoral Thesis" 1998). Obviously that's unacceptable, so the question is not *whether* we will do something about current costs but *what* we will do and *when* and *how* we will do it.

This subject, then, is simply a brief expression of some concepts and practices bringing to light the underlying cause of our health care dilemma. It is not one of a technical presentation of facts or data but rather an *ethical* expression, if you will, in an effort to speak out boldly on some moral and social issues too often ignored by many in the health care arena. It is, in fact, a presentation of conflicts among competing values.

Consider the following scenario: Mr. Johnson is seventy-eight years old and in the intensive care unit at City Hospital. He has been saved from death seven times in the past eighteen months, each time receiving massive transfusions to replace the blood lost in his abdomen as a result of alcoholic liver disease. In addition, he has cancer of the esophagus, which could cause his death within a few months. His problem is fairly common in ICUs. This is the thirty-seventh day of intensive care for this hospitalization. In the past eighteen months, his ICU stays total ninety-eight days, resulting in a hospital bill in excess of $400,000, much of which has been paid by Medicare. Each hospitalization was precipitated by a period of heavy drinking. Would it be wrong to limit Mr. Johnson to three hospitalizations for gastrointestinal bleeding due to alcoholism? After three hospital stays, would it be morally permissible to provide *only* comfort care and allow him to die? Consider the following moral judgment: people who abuse their health should have less claim on expensive life-prolonging medical care than those who have taken good care of themselves. Would you endorse that judgment? How would your judgment concerning Mr. Thompson change if there were only nine beds in the ICU and he was among three patients waiting for the ninth bed? What criteria should determine who occupies the last available bed? What is the policy here? This is a dilemma haunting today's health care system. It is happening all over.

According to latest data by CMS (Centers for Medicare & Medical Services), national health care expenditures rose 5.3 percent in 2014 to $3 trillion, or $9,523 per person. The numbers are higher today, but actual numbers are not readily available due to changing policies in the health care arena. This gives an idea of how expensive health care in the US is getting. The Congressional Budget Office (CBO) claims this is about 17 percent of the gross national product. Whereas the cost of other goods and services has increased in single digits in the past fifteen years, the cost of health care is about ten times what it was about twenty years ago; this is my estimation. For example, in 1990, General Motors spent more money on health care for its employees than it spent on steel to make their cars ("Critical Issues in American Health Care—Doctoral Thesis"). It is no wonder, then, why the automobile industry needed a bailout from the government to save it. Remember that one?

There are several factors that contribute to this situation. These are: the duplication of services, waste, excessive paperwork, malpractice costs, the expensive nature of research, the expensive development of new drugs and medical equipment, and the gross misuse of funds. A major factor determining the high cost of health care is the increasing demand for enhanced quality care. Americans have come to expect miracles from medicine, turning health care into a consumer product like soft drinks, videos, or cars. Nowadays, health care professionals have reached a point where they're trying to define the term "quality" in the quest to deliver cost-effective care. But the major factor contributing to the high cost of health care is the increased demand for care resulting from *careless* living—that is, unhealthy and immoral lifestyles. Overall, it is the greed of doctors, pharmaceutical companies, and insurance companies and the recklessness of patients that is causing skyrocketing health care costs. People live as they please and expect medicine to fix the consequences. However, medicine is not always the answer.

For example, several years ago, when I arrived at my credit union to take care of some personal business, I witnessed a fire truck and an EMS ambulance parked in front of the entrance. The EMS techs were administering medical care to a grossly obese man who appeared to have passed out. He was already recovering (or coming to) but was still very pale. In his shirt pocket was a pack of cigarettes. I don't know the details of this man's ailments or health, but it would not surprise me to discover that this man was suffering from some type of heart or pulmonary disease.

I do know that his gross weight and the smoking of cigarettes greatly contributed to his apparent ill health. (Note: according to recent reports by the American Lung Association, cigarette smoking causes more than 480,000 deaths each year in the United States, nearly one in five deaths.) Along his side, very frightened and confused, was his wife. She also was obese and by all means did not have the appearance of a healthy woman. Yet these people expected to be taken care of. In terms of resources, we must consciously consider the cost to administer medical aid and probable hospitalization in cases such as these. Should medical care have been denied in this case? Or is medical care an entitlement everyone should have, regardless of their style of life? One side of me says no, they should not be denied. Everyone should get emergent medical attention no matter what. The other side of me says the opposite—that is, people who make their bed must sleep in it. Is it a question of compassion versus apathy? Or is it a question of just plain responsibility? What's the policy in this case? Whatever our views may be, these things should raise our consciousness about the allocation of health care.

There is a growing belief in society that health care rationing is inescapable; no amount of effort to eliminate waste and inefficiency in the health care system will change this fact. Rationing has already begun in some states, where a basic standard of medical care is guaranteed to all citizens. But this oftentimes means that the overall standard is lowered in order to accommodate greater numbers of people, particularly those not covered by private insurance.

Given the current emphasis upon individual rights and personal autonomy, it is not surprising that the claim to a right to health care has secured a stronghold on the public consciousness. Health care is considered morally special, unlike other commodities in society. The inability to pay should not exclude anyone from receiving treatment, particularly if we value individual human life. This sounds good but is unrealistic in a world that demands payment for services rendered, especially at a time when the economy is unstable.

Others believe that no one should receive what they cannot pay for, that to appropriate someone else's money to pay for one's own health care constitutes an infringement of that person's rights. Human life, according to this view, is not priceless, and there are limits to what society ought to spend on saving or extending life through medical intervention. Those who hold this view say it is immoral to take other people's money to give expensive, life-extending care to someone who cannot pay for it him/ herself, especially when their ill-health is the result of careless living. I dare say, they have a valid point.

Let's look at a more sensitive issue here. Supposedly, it is wrong to take, let's say, $400,000 from the health care pool in a health maintenance organization (HMO) to provide an extra six months of life for a patient dying from AIDS contracted by homosexual activity. The latter view holds that not all human life is worthy of maximal efforts at preservation. The quality of life supersedes the morality of life. Therefore, an AIDS patient has lesser rights to health care resources than someone with heart disease. The principle supporting this view is *justice*. Health resources are finite. For whom should they be reserved? Who decides who receives which resources? Our society maintains no consensus of justice, so the answer is left to the most vocal and the most organized, which is hardly just. So the issue here is morality versus justice, or vice versa. Who wins? The majority may win, but the majority may not be right.

We see the principle of justice at work in other arenas (or so we think). For example, all of us have a limited right to police and fire protection, whether we pay taxes or not. We are protected by the military from foreign attack regardless of whether we pay income taxes or have served in the armed services. That is because society values human life highly enough to *assume* that we deserve protection. However, that right is not absolute, because it would be impossible to provide universal twenty-four-hour police and fire protection unless the nation was transformed into a police state. One's claim to police or fire protection increases as the threat increases. It is impossible to provide an armed guard for every citizen since resources are limited. But if an intruder enters your home and threatens your life, your claim to police protection increases dramatically. A person receiving death threats has more of a claim to police protection than someone whose neighbor's dog is barking. In other words, the greater the threat, the greater the claim, and it is all based upon a principle of justice. Get the point here?

If we accept the premise that health resources are finite, perhaps their allocation must be determined according to the same concept of justice. Under this principle, neither caregivers nor patients would be able to make unlimited demands on hospitals or other public resources, especially in regard to futile or marginally beneficial or purely elective medical procedures. Tummy tucks, face lifts, and nontherapeutic cosmetic surgeries may be limited or eliminated altogether in order for those resources to be used in a more just manner. Likewise, organ transplants, fertility treatments, or other expensive, life-extending treatments that offer only marginal prospect of benefit to a patient may also be limited or eliminated in order for medical resources to be offered to someone who could receive more benefit from them.

Given the depravity of humanity, it is difficult for individuals to make fair allocation decisions about their own health care, especially if they are poor or prone to poor health. It is also hard to imagine care providers making completely just allocation decisions, even within the confines of a national health insurance program. Although the aim of socialized medicine (an unpopular term) is to provide basic health care for everyone, its effect may be that the standard of health care is reduced. The real reason President Clinton's health care reform plan did not pass in the 1990s, and the reason Obamacare is very unpopular, is because both are indicative of a socialized system. And in a free-enterprise system, such a system is just not acceptable. However, this is not to say that in the not too distant future the options or choices will not be exhausted; the inevitable is clear. But the predominant issue under socialized systems is whether the state will pay for it, not whether the patient or care provider agrees to it. This clashes with what we traditionally are accustomed to, and that is a free-enterprise system.

Another view is that economics directly affect the capabilities of any society to either produce or consume. In the past, physicians controlled most health care resources and were free to allocate them for their patients' use. Today, many health care resources are controlled by the government, large corporations, and managed care entities, with physicians acting as mere employees. Consequently, physicians are in the unique position of appropriating other people's resources for their patients, whether the patients have the ability to pay for them or not. Some would call that a form of theft, a type of benevolent expropriation or redistribution of wealth, and a strong argument against this is this: in taking away physicians' ability to allocate resources for their patients, the physician is no longer an uncompromised advocate for the patient's best interests. This, in a sense, is a great blow to the patient and to the integrity of the medical profession. By forcing doctors to seek approval to use resources, we may subject them to the whims of bureaucratic, cost-cutting policies and cumbersome decision-making procedures. On the other hand, managed care practices have proven to produce quality medical care and significant cost-cutting results in the delivery of health care. Which of the lesser evils do we choose?

If economics are to be the sole standard for allocating medical care, health care will become simply another part of a market economy of goods and services. That will work against the likelihood of maintaining a strong sanctity of life ethic and a healthy lifestyle. It should be noted that the tremendous cost of health care is, at least in part, due to the fact that higher prices are already charged to those with the ability to pay in order to cover the costs of those who can't. But picking up the tab for someone else doesn't solve the problem. If access to health care were determined solely by one's ability to pay, it is possible that costs would decrease somewhat. However, it would still not solve the problem, because governments, like markets, sometimes fail to promote the social good. It would hardly make up for society's loss in those who would die for lack of medical care. Unlike consumer products, medical care is morally special. It cannot be compared with owning a car or home. The sick can attest to this fact, in that without good health, nothing else matters much. The ability or inability to pay should not be the lone factor in allocating health care resources; rather, the actual circumstances of each particular case should be the determining factors.

As a society, we are still in the early stages of the debate over the allocation of health care resources. There are many questions that still do not have answers. We cannot accurately predict the exact consequences of these trials and tribulations, but perhaps the true solution to all this lies in the responsibility for one to exercise a healthier and moral lifestyle. This is an area only the bold dare to address. The truth is we are a fat, irresponsible, and sick nation. We've neglected our health and abused our bodies. We are continuously and carelessly exhausting those systems designed to care for us, and the ramifications are now taking a serious toll on all of us. Don't believe this? Look at your insurance premiums. In times when our own government cannot even balance the budget, we must be aware of our personal failures if we are to avoid the most ineffective and unwise interferences with private choices. It is not that we don't know what is right or wrong but rather that we've rejected doing the right things. If priorities and allocations were focused on wellness incentives, rather than on efforts in the overwhelming task of curing everyone, there is no doubt we could considerably avert the uncontrollable costs of health care. It's like the rising gas pump prices. Do you know why they are high and continue to rise? Because we pay them. Because we're weak. We give in to the pleasures of our desires. We are a spoiled people. That overweight soccer mom in her vehicle full of brats, with her cell phone stuck to her ears while she's driving, running stoplights and stop signs, is part of the problem, an accident waiting to happen, and it does. Did I offend anyone? What's more offensive is ending up in the trauma room or the morgue, statistics you don't hear about very often, until you see it on the local news that evening, or someone in your family is a casualty of such an accident. Reality then sets in. Where's the health care here?

Here's the thing. This nation has the capacity, in terms of resources, knowledge, and ability, to assure every citizen access to the highest-quality health care ever known to humankind. That we have not done so is not necessarily a reflection of our lack of caring for one another but rather, in part, a manifestation of our pluralistic/judicial system and bureaucratic overload. Let me educate everyone: health care is a commodity, like gas or oil. Either you can afford it or you can't. It is not a right or even a privilege, like many want to believe. It is an entitlement that has been earned. Until the pharmaceuticals, the hospitals, and insurance companies are brought under control, all efforts to improve it are futile. It is complicated, yes, but they've made it complicated. The more complicated it is, the more profit for those causing this ... complication.

Health care is a vital and personal concern of every American, and it is a major concern of national policy makers. Because the problems in health care are wide and complex, they must be faced and dealt with great wisdom and personal commitment by everyone involved in this arena. We no longer have the luxury of doing our own thing and expecting others to take care of our problems. The time has come to take control of our lives and our personal health. Failure to do so will invite the empirical reality of others to decide what's best for us. That is, we will be required to be submissive to those managing our medical resources, and that, gentlemen and ladies, is vehemently unacceptable!

"It is not the healthy who need a doctor,
but the sick."
—Matthew 9:12

The only real alternative to health is … death.
—(aah)

CHAPTER 4

Immigration and the Alien

The Problem with Immigrants

This is the next problem I want to address. It is a sensitive one that is dividing our country, causing hate and havoc, one that has the potential to destroy us, within ourselves.

On February 4, 2013, Russian president Vladimir Putin gave a powerful speech to Duma (Russian Parliament). Here's what he said (read this carefully): "In Russia live Russians. Any minority, from anywhere, if it wants to live in Russia, to work and eat in Russia, should speak Russian, and should respect the Russian laws. If they prefer Sharia Law, then we advise them to go to those places where that's the state law. Russia does not need minorities. Minorities need Russia, and we will not grant them special privileges, or try to change our laws to fit their desires, no matter how loud they yell 'discrimination.' We'd better learn from the suicides of America, England, Holland and France, if we are to survive as a nation. The Russian customs and traditions are not compatible with the lack of culture or the primitive ways of most minorities. When this honorable legislative body thinks of creating new laws, it should have in mind the national interest first, observing that the minorities are not Russians." The politicians in the Duma gave Putin a standing ovation. Now, I'm no fan of Mr. Putin, but he has a viable point here. Sometimes we can learn from our enemies.

As we struggle with the immigration problem in this country, maybe we can learn something from Putin. That is, America too must understand that our customs and traditions are not compatible with those of other nationalities. We can no longer afford other cultures invading ours. The attack on the Boston Marathon proved that. Two Russian immigrants were allowed in our country, lived here for years, were even given rights to benefits, and no one ever really questioned their immigration status. They came here with the intent to kill Americans. They did just that. As usual, people got very upset and patriotic. But nothing changed. Immigration got more complex. Thousands of women and children continued to come from Latin countries, flooding our borders and homeland. The question that should be raised is, Where are the men, the husbands and fathers of these women and children? What about the governments of these countries? One American senator said, "Put them in a bus or a plane back to their country." To some, this may sound cruel. Really? Are you willing to foot the bill through your tax dollars for the welfare of these illegal immigrants? I'm not. I've got enough problems paying my bills. I don't have the means to support someone else's irresponsibility. Do you?

The avalanche of thousands of women and children coming from foreign countries, flooding our borders and occupying our homeland, is now of paramount concern. Yes, we are a compassionate people. It's what separates us from the rest of the world. We go to war for others only to discover later that we may have blundered. As a Vietnam War veteran, I know something about this.

At some point, we must draw the line. Let me reiterate: are we willing to foot the bill through our tax dollars for the irresponsibility of the husbands, fathers, and governments of these women and children? We have our own problems. We have seniors, veterans, the homeless, and sick children (i.e., children's hospitals) of our own to care for. We have weather disasters destroying everything people worked hard for all their lives. We have infrastructures that need urgent attention. We have mass shootings in our cities. Our government is dysfunctional, our country divided. There is chaos all over. We don't need someone else's problems. I cannot stress this enough.

Those who came here illegally and knowingly did so are now paying the price. It is not a pleasant thing to see families torn apart due to deportation practices. But unfortunately, that's the law. Maybe the laws need to be changed. This is where our political representatives and leaders must take charge. It is easy to feel sorry for the immigrant or the Dreamer. What's hard is the law.

I was once an immigrant myself. I came here at the age of six. I quickly learned English. Went to school here, in El Paso, Texas. Graduated from high school. Went to Vietnam. Came back. I still had to apply for my citizenship. I officially became an American citizen in 1969. Going to war for this country did not qualify you for automatic citizenship. I still had to go through the difficult process. There was no special program for me like DACA. I earned my citizenship in compliance with immigration law. My younger brother came close to being deported because he had not become a citizen. He had been here many years, had a family and home, held several jobs. Paid taxes. Did not have a criminal record. He was a good man, husband, and father. All of that did not matter. He was on the verge of being deported. He was given a year to become a citizen. He died before he could become a citizen. He came very close to being a victim of current immigration law. My mother faced the same situation. But she too died before the laws caught up to her. I remember telling both of them many years ago, urging them to apply for citizenship. As for me, I'm now an American. I am *not* an immigrant. While I have fond memories of Mexico and family there, America is my country. English is my language. The Bible is my religion. *That* makes me an American.

The ideology of admitting just anyone into our country is not representative of true immigration law and procedures. I know this from studying immigration law. But today, immigrants are coming in from all fronts. They are flooding our borders and invading our homeland. They are demanding benefits and privileges they have not earned. The nation of Islam is polluting our country with millions of Muslims. Radical Islamists are bringing to America another god called Allah and demanding we put aside the God of Abraham, Isaac, and Jacob. School districts in America are providing prayer rooms for Islamic students, yet Christians are not allowed to pray in our schools. Something is wrong with this picture!

We have seen the horror of radical Islamists in the mass killings of

The Audacity of Truth

Americans by Muslims. Recently on *60 Minutes,* a young Muslim man was interviewed because he was caught trying to join ISIS. He was planning on killing more Americans. He was already here, as a citizen. He openly confessed that it was out of obedience to Allah. He's facing life imprisonment and doesn't care because he's doing it for Allah. Another Muslim, Abdul Razak Ali Artan, shot and stabbed ten students at Ohio State University. He was considered a terrorist. The most recent one (at this writing) was in Manhattan, New York, on October 31, 2017. He killed eight and injured eleven. It was the worst terrorist attack since 9/11, according to the mayor of New York. The nation was once again shaken.

The truth is the alien is in our backyard trying to take over. And he (or she) will do so at any cost because, according to their religion, to die for Allah by killing Americans is their mission and is the pathway to their heaven. In our schools right now, a Muslim can practice their faith without question, but if a Christian gets caught praying or reading the Bible, they will get in trouble. A Christian teacher in California was fired because she led her class in prayer and a Muslim student complained. In our military, mosques have been built for their worship, and Muslims are allowed to carry the Koran (their bible). But if a soldier, a marine, a sailor, or an airman gets caught praying or reading the Bible in public, they can be reprimanded. Why? Because it is offensive to Muslims. This is a fact, and it is happening today. Why? Because we have allowed the alien to enter our country for the sake of political correctness, which is killing the spirit of this country. Politicians will tell us that the attacks on our people by Muslims is not about religion. Bull! That's exactly what it's about. They want Allah in and Christ out. Some (even some ministers) will argue the "freedom of religion." The freedom of religion was never meant to allow a foreign nation to come here and practice their faith by attacking our people and imposing their religious beliefs on us. The freedom of speech and religion (First Amendment) was written so that we, as Christians, could worship and profess the true God of the Bible without persecution by unbelievers. The freedom of religion clause has been grossly taken out of context. George Washington, our first president and forefather of our nation, said, "It is impossible to rightly govern a nation without God and the Bible." John Adams said, "I have examined all religions, and the result is that the Bible is the best book in the world." Patrick Henry said, "There is a book [the Bible] worth all the other books ever printed." Franklin D. Roosevelt said, "The United States is founded on the principles of Christianity." Ronald Reagan said, "We will never abandon our belief in God." "The Congress of the United States approves the first Holy Bible in America" (United States Congress, 1782). "This is a Christian nation" (United States Supreme Court decision in *Church of the Holy Trinity v. United States*, 1982). Our previous president (Obama) said, "Whatever we once were, we are no longer a Christian nation." Wrong, Mr. President! Our nation *is* a Christian nation. It was formed on the basis of Christianity. It was written on Christian principles. To deviate from this is to invite God's wrath. The book of Deuteronomy in the Old Testament tells us of the blessings and curses concerning our obedience and disobedience to God:

> "If you fully obey the Lord your God and carefully follow all His commands, I give you today, the Lord your God will set you high above all the nations on earth … However, if you do not obey the Lord your God and do not carefully follow all His commands and decrees I am giving you today, all these curses will come upon you and overtake you." (Deuteronomy 28:1–15.

We must understand that countries have changed, governments have changed, people have changed. The world has changed; 9/11 changed everything. It changed us. What should not change is our American image. A woman wearing a shield hiding her face and under brutal submission by her husband is not an American. A man wearing a taqiya is not an American. A person waving the Mexican flag and constantly complaining about our country is not an American. A professional football player refusing to stand for the national anthem and respect the flag is not an American. These are *not* Americans. We have allowed the alien to enter our homeland and pollute our American culture. We have allowed them to live here, plotting to kill us. We are *not* a nation of immigrants. We are a nation of Americans. The melting pot days are long over. We need to get over this immigration paranoia. It is killing us, literally. It is causing hate and discontent. It is killing the American spirit. I say this not in hate, for that would be a damnable sin. I say it in truth and conviction, to save our beloved country. We, this generation, will perish someday, as our days are numbered. What will we leave our children, our grandchildren? What kind of country will they inherit? These are the things we should be thinking about, talking about, and doing something about. This is America. We are Americans, not Muslims, not Mexicans, not Africans. The world knows us as Americans. Nothing else.

"The alien who lives among you will rise above you
higher and higher, but you will sink lower and lower.
He will lend to you, but you will not lend to him.
He will be the head, but you will be the tail."
—Deuteronomy 28:43–44 NKJV

The basis of all wars is ... religion.
—(aah)

CHAPTER 5

War and Terror

Imminent War and Terror

We have watched the horror of innocent children killed by their own government. We have watched the firing of American missiles at a country in chaos and the dropping of the largest bomb ever, both with little results, if any. We have heard the hostile responses by Iran and Russia: "We will not allow US to dominate the world." We have watched the political fiasco concerning immigration, health care, and a dystopian government.

We have watched and heard about the North Korean crisis, tensions escalating each day. We are not winning in Afghanistan or in Iraq. What makes us think we can win against a determined enemy that has an army of over a million, an air force, a navy, and nuclear weapons? We have an all-volunteer force; they're trained since childhood. They have warned us: "Do not provoke us." How much more do we have to see and hear? I'm talking about North Korea.

We are just one reckless decision away from a major and total war. Our military and VA hospitals are already overwhelmed. Are we ready for the casualty count? At what price are we willing to wage another war to satisfy our psychotic paranoia? All these are signs of a very bad outcome.

In the area of terror, terrorists don't have to take over the United States or even slaughter millions of people in order to win the fight. All they have to do is slowly paralyze or disrupt various aspects of American life-as-usual style, and they win. A country doesn't have to be defeated militarily. It can be defeated psychologically or economically. The 9/11 attacks accomplished just that.

A country can be defeated by driving the people to a paranoiac state of mind that can cause it to react in irrational ways. The terrorists know this, so they do the one thing they know they can do—terrorize us. When we get to the point where we start making our elderly American citizens go through x-ray machines and embarrassing them by exposing their age-old bodies, we've already been defeated. When you can't get to work on time because of extensive and aggressive search procedures by obnoxious security employees, we've been defeated. When you fear going to a mall or a concert, we've been defeated. When Americans live in fear every day of another terrorist attack, we've been defeated. It's a psychological war, and we're losing.

The only realistic chance to win the war against terrorism is to go directly to the source and annihilate them. There is no other way. All other efforts are futile. Many argue that too many innocents would die. What about those three thousand that were killed in 9/11? What were they? What about the four thousand plus American troops that have lost their lives in Iraq due to 9/11, a war we erroneously rushed into and are still fighting? In WWII, we dropped two atomic bombs on two Japanese cities in order to win the war and save thousands of American lives. Innocent women and children died instantly. It was, yes, a terrible way to win. But we had to. Many years later, there was a movement in this country to apologize to the people of Japan for such a horrific action. But no one was ever asked to apologize for Pearl Harbor. It was a brutal and merciless attack. Over three thousand sailors and marines died that Day of Infamy (December 7, 1941). And, what about the 58,000-plus that died in Vietnam, for nothing? Let's think about that the next time we feel sorry for other countries that want to destroy us; yes, think about that.

Those given the awful task of combat must be able to act with the necessary savagery and purposefulness to destroy those who want to destroy us. Human behavior has not changed much in recorded history.

Neither have the basic tenets of war. It takes killing with speed and sustained effect to win wars. The famous army general George S. Patton said, "You don't win a war by dying for your country, you win it by making the other dumb bastard die for his country." Strong words by an American general. But he was right. President Harry S. Truman did not flinch to drop the two atomic bombs on Japan. He did it to win World War II and saved thousands of American lives. This is the mentality that we need to fight our wars and the war on terror.

Until we destroy the enemy at their home, we can expect more of these attacks at our homeland. Recent events have confirmed this. The question is not whether or not it will happen; rather, it's when and where. That's a hell of way to live, don't you think?

For by wise counsel you will wage your own war ...
—Proverbs 24:6 NIV

Consider the source. Then destroy it.
—(aah)

CHAPTER 6

My Vietnam Story

Albert A. Hernandez
US Navy Hospital Corpsman—HM2
Combat Medic, Vietnam, '66–67

This one is about me. I graduated from Jefferson High School in May 1965, in El Paso, Texas. Shortly after graduation, I received a letter telling me to report to the reception station for my physical. I was on the verge of being drafted into the military. Immediately I went to the navy recruiting office and enlisted. I always wanted to be a sailor anyway. I did not want to get drafted by the army or the marines. I didn't want to end up in Vietnam. The Vietnam War was starting to get intense. The casualty count was rising. Young boys were getting killed. I was nineteen when I enlisted.

I reported to boot camp and underwent twelve weeks of brutal training. Navy boot camp in those days was hard. They kicked your ass, called you names I can't print. After completing boot camp, I reported to Navy Hospital Corps School in San Diego, California. I was assigned to be a Navy Hospital corpsman (medic). It was sixteen weeks of intensive study and training in the area of medicine and patient care, experience that would shape my future. I was then assigned to the Balboa Naval Hospital in San Diego. I worked in the wards for exactly six months. I worked all three shifts. I know what it is to work in a hospital. It's no picnic either. Then came the shocker: I was drafted to the Fleet Marine Force (FMF).

In October 1966, I reported to Medical Service School in Camp Pendleton, California, to be trained as a combat medic with the grunts (marines). Navy corpsmen serve as medics to the marines. It was six weeks of grueling training. FMF training was tough. They get you in top physical shape. You learn how to handle the various weapons. You practice field medicine for the casualties. It was scary because it exposed you to the reality of war; in other words, I was on my way to war.

I deployed to Vietnam in December 1967. It was a bleak time for my family and me. My mother and little brother saw me off at the airport. My mom could not stop crying. She gave me the blessing of the cross on my forehead. I'll never forget that. There is nothing like the blessing of a mother.

There are many events I think about from my Vietnam experience, but there is one in particular I must tell about. While on a company patrol, I got sick. Not to give our position away, I was directed by the company commander to go to the nearest camp that was about three miles down the road and railroad tracks. I was told to follow the tracks that would lead me to an army outfit. As I walked alone, I kept thinking about what would happen to me if the enemy spotted me. I was scared. Every step I took was in fear. I would be no match for the enemy. As corpsmen, your only weapon is a .45-caliber pistol. It's for self-defense only. When I got to the army camp, they were amazed that I had walked that distance alone without being spotted. I have to believe I was not alone. My guardian angel was with me. The hand of God was over me. Yes, I believe very much in God. I made it to safety. I could have easily been killed that day.

There were many close calls and days when I was sure I was not going to make it. After about two hundred patrols and three major operations, I survived. In the last operation, my company got hit real hard. I was the only corpsman alive! It was not my time. These events inspired me to write a paper years ago for *Veterans' Voices* magazine, "Not My Time." It was published nationally. It made the coversheet. People at the VA, where I retired from, read it. They know who I am when I walk through the doors of the El Paso VA where I get my health care.

But not all of it was combat. As a corpsman, I rendered care not only to our marines but also to the Vietnamese people. The infant in a village suffering from multiple head infections is a heartbreaking memory I'll never forget. We would go to the villages to treat the sick. It was a compassionate duty that we performed while there. It was, for me, the only thing that I can truly say I liked because I met people there who appreciated what we did. The father of the infant I treated offered me his young daughter in appreciation for the care to his infant son. Of course I could not accept. By the way, we saw some very beautiful Vietnamese girls in Vietnam. That's all I'll say about that.

I completed my navy enlistment in 1978. I was medically discharged due to knee problems. As a corpsman, my MOS (military occupational specialty) was HM-8404, meaning combat medic. Because of my knee problems, I was no longer fit to remain in the navy, so I had to get discharged. In those days, if you were not physically fit, they discharged you. The strain of my tour in Vietnam took its toll on me, in more ways than one. Nevertheless, I have been awarded the appropriate medals. In fact, I am considered a highly decorated Vietnam War veteran. I served my country valiantly and honorably, and I apologize to no one. In Vietnam, we did the best we could.

My Vietnam experience made me stronger. It taught me not to give up. Life is too precious. I've been spared by the Almighty. That is "My Vietnam Story."

Note: This story was incorporated in the Vietnam Digital Wall Album in 2017 at El Paso, Texas.

> And we know that all things work together for good
> to those who love God, to those who are
> the called according to His
> purpose.
> —Romans 8:28 NKJV

> Ask not what your country can do for you; ask what you
> can do for your country.
> —John F. Kennedy

CHAPTER 7

The Wrath Within

A Dormant Anger in Us All

We've seen it as "the war within," PTSD, and other relevant titles, describing what the Vietnam War veteran and others went through. We've seen countless movies showing what this war was about. Countless documentaries have played on the television airwaves showing the public what it was about and why. But today, I wish to present it as it really is: "The Wrath Within." The word "wrath" is defined in *Webster's Dictionary* as "intense anger; rage; fury; any action carried out in great anger, esp. for punishment or vengeance." In the Bible, it is mentioned many times, mostly as the "wrath of God" against a corrupt, cruel, and sinful world.

Recently, I saw on the History Channel a documentary called *Vietnam in HD*. It was about the Vietnam War, a war I was in. At first, I was reluctant to see it because I was afraid it might set off my emotions about the war. But then I thought, *Wait a minute, I was there. I had to see if they told it like it was, you know, the "truth."* They did. The footage was graphic. The scenes were real. My wife saw parts of it. I said to her, "See that? See that? That's what I did. That's what I saw. That's what I went through!" She kept asking me if I was okay. I said yes, but I wasn't. I had to watch it. My wife knows me. She knows how I get when I hear or see something about the Vietnam War. She saw what I went through when I worked for the VA. In the VA, I held a high position in management. I saw and learned a lot. I saw the politics and bureaucracy of it. But I was also able to help many veterans. My desire was to help those who were hurting and suffering. There was a divine reason I was spared in that war. But in October 2006, I finally had to retire due to my own health reasons. It was tough for me. I didn't want to leave. But that day, when I ended up in the emergency room, my VA doctor told me it was time to retire. I was told I came close to having a heart attack or a stroke. It was a warning sign. Retirement had not been in my plans. But when your body tells you otherwise, the choice is no longer yours. No matter how strong you think you are, life and war eventually take their toll on you. Don't believe this? The cemeteries are full of unbelievers.

That day, I recall, I was angry. Very angry. Is this what I went to war for? Did I survive a war and thirty-six years of federal service for this? Is this what Vietnam vets died for? When I see what's going on in the world today and the dirty politics going on in Washington, it enrages me. When I see on TV that casket with the American flag draped over it, I am angered. When I hear that politicians want to cut our benefits, it boils my blood. My wife has to calm me down. I take my medication and go to bed. It's how I deal with this rage that's in me. On the bumper sticker of a vet's car, it read: "Vietnam Vet: DFWM!" I'm sure you can figure out the acronym. But that is how many war vets really feel. They're angry. It's a hidden anger that's hard to describe. It is a wrath you can't simply get rid of with drugs or therapy. It is, in fact, a dangerous way of living. Maybe that's why suicide deaths amongst veterans are on the rise, but that's another story for another time, and I have much to say about that.

"Vietnam vet with PTSD kills wife and children" was the headline news on local television one day. What caused this veteran to kill his family? His family! Later, as more details were uncovered by the media, it was revealed that this veteran was unable to find work, benefits were denied, and the care at the VA was poor. This man was suffering and hurting. He needed help and attention. No one cared. No one saw it coming because they didn't want to see it. He was just "another veteran with an attitude problem" or simply another statistic. That's how many vets are perceived. But a young woman and her two children died that day. I think that's more than just an attitude problem or a number, don't you? But that's the reality today. Vets are taking their lives and those of others. That shooter that killed twenty-five people in a Texas church was an angry man. Anger needs no motive. Anger is not limited to war veterans. Anyone can have this hidden, silent wrath. Anyone. Even, yes, you!

So, what's the problem here? Why are people angry? Here are a few reasons. We've been lied to about Vietnam. We've been lied to about Iraq and Afghanistan. We've been lied to about health care. We've been lied to about radical Islam, which intends to destroy America. We've given billions of dollars to countries that want to destroy us. We are helping sponsor terrorism in the Middle East by giving these hostile nations our money. We are taking in people from other countries and neglecting our own. These are facts and not just my opinion. These are the issues of the times that raise anger and frustration. Those mass shootings in our schools are caused by people who are angry and have lost control of themselves.

Now comes the NFL players who are refusing to honor the American flag, whose existence was purchased with rivers of American blood by soldiers and marines who gave their last full measure of devotion to keep it flying, that we may be free. It's amazing to me that these athletes make millions protecting a football while our soldiers and marines get a pittance protecting our country.

The rage I carry is an anger that torments me almost every day. When I see what's going on in my country, it breaks my heart. Every day, I hear or see something bad or wicked happening. Turn on the TV, and all you get is bad news. All you see is filth and trash, programs that are polluting the minds of our kids. We can thank the media for that; they're experts at feeding our society cyanide poison with their relentless reporting that focuses mostly on evil and wicked things. Political correctness has replaced common sense. Then we wonder why that mass shooting at a school or church happened; why our policemen are being attacked and ambushed; why our government is so dysfunctional, and so on. The devil has taken a foothold on the very soul of this country. Today's younger generation are called millennials. They haven't a clue what it really means to be an American, much less the price to be one. But they do know they have the right to protest against the very country that gives them that right. In other countries, you can go directly to jail if you burn the flag or protest against the government; no lawyer or jury, just jail. In some cases, you can be executed.

These are the things that boil my blood. Maybe I've seen too much. Maybe it's because in Vietnam I saw too many men and young boys die for our country and that flag that many want to dishonor and burn. I was only nineteen when I went to war. I wasn't even old enough to drink alcohol legally here in my own country. But I went. I obeyed the law. And I don't care how many doctors I see or how much medication I take, or how much religion I believe in, the mental trauma and anger are still there.

Today's current events don't help. Right now, as I write this book, we're on the brink of war that will affect every American. We have watched as tensions with North Korea escalate. We have watched the horror of innocent children killed by their own country. We have watched a president change his mind about his campaign promises and blatantly lie to us. We have watched the firing of American missiles at a country already in chaos. We have watched the dropping of the largest bomb ever, with no real results, just more innocents killed. We have heard the hostile responses by our enemy countries, Iran and Russia: "We will not allow the US to dominate the world" (a quote per a CNN report). We have heard the American ambassador suggesting more military action, not realizing the ramifications of war. The secretary of State stated that the policy of strategic patience is over and all options are on the table, meaning imminent war. Our health care system is a mess, with our military and VA hospitals already overwhelmed. Are we ready for the casualty count? All these are signs of a very bad outcome.

But who am I, what am I, to feel this way, to say these strong words? I am an American citizen and a war veteran. I've paid my dues. No one gave me anything. I had to earn what I have. But as I said before, I am also grateful. I live in a country that at least gives you the right to have the things you desire, the freedom to write what you feel is just and righteous. I don't believe in being poor, in America. I refuse to be destitute. But take my rights away, and I'll give you a war you won't believe. That's the wrath within.

> "But I am full of the wrath of the Lord,
> and I cannot hold it in."
> —Jeremiah 6:11

> Anger needs no motive.
> —(aah)

Chapter 8

God and the VA

The Veterans Administration

This is a personal testimonial of my working experience while employed at the El Paso VA Health Care System, a VA outpatient clinic here in El Paso, Texas. It is mainly for the glory of God and for the sake of all medical facilities. I hope and pray that it will be read because I feel it sets the precedence for the following subjects, and there is a moral and spiritual imperative in this message for all of us. Every word of it is true and in the fear of the Lord.

I started working at the El Paso VA in June 1999. I remember how excited I was when I found out that I had gotten the position of administrative assistant to the chief of staff (AA/COS) there at the VA. It is normally considered a very high and prestigious position in the area of clinical management in the VAs. I also remember people at William Beaumont Army Medical Center (WBAMC), where I was previously employed as a health systems specialist and supervisor, telling me I would never get that position because it was too political and they probably already had somebody hand-picked for it. I accepted the position because it was a promotion, and according to the job description, it was tailor-made for me. I had always wanted to work for the VA so that I could help veterans.

Everybody was stunned when I gave them the news and said that I would be leaving in about two weeks. You see, I was a supervisor at WBAMC. I supervised three major areas consisting of about eighteen employees. They hated to see me go. My supervisor, an army LTC, was very upset when he found out I was leaving. He said, "Why didn't you tell me? I would have promoted you." I replied, "I did, but you didn't listen to me. Instead, you gave me more work and responsibility." I remember these words well. Get the picture so far?

After reporting to the VA, I found out later that some people there thought I would not last very long because my predecessor was there only about two years and resigned due to the extreme stress of the job. The AA/COS position in the VA is a demanding job. It's not for just anyone. I guess they saw me as too meek and probably weak. But what they didn't know was that I was a fighter and a man of God.

I was not like anyone else. One person actually told me that I was there for a purpose. She could see that in me. She knew something. During my tenure there, I demonstrated exceptional performance. The director would sometimes give me special assignments. This clashed with my supervisor, who was possessive and an extreme micromanager. But I thought, *That's okay.* I was tougher, smarter, and organized. I quickly learned that they didn't know what they were doing, and that's why they were having many problems. People gradually became aware of my credentials and my abilities. My status as a Vietnam War veteran became well known, but they still didn't realize the other side of me. They didn't realize I was a man of God. A few, I dare say, found out the hard way because "If God is for us, who can be against us?" (Romans 8:31).

Then one day, I was asked to give the invocation and benediction in one of the special ceremonies held at the VA. I was frequently asked to do this when we would have special events, such as for POWs/MIAs, Veterans' Day, Christmas, and other festivities that the VA would honor. It was a high privilege for me, as this is where God used me big-time in the VA. I recall one doctor telling me, "You are our minister." I was profoundly moved by that statement because it came from one of our most respected and valued physicians, who, to our misfortune, later resigned. In another special event, in which I was asked again to give the invocation and benediction, a senior executive in management told me not to mention the Lord's name "Jesus" in my prayer. I was upset about that. So I didn't. It affected me very much. I asked God for forgiveness. Shortly after that, this man who told me to do that suddenly started having serious problems at work. He almost lost his job. He was suspended for months, as I recall. He was a mess. While most were judging him, I was praying for him. Many thought he would never return. Well, he did return. He returned at the mercy of the director and, I believe, my prayers too. But it was never the same for him. When you denounce the Lord, your life will change ... for the worse.

I hung in there for a total of seven years. I went through many trials there. But God used me, as I always treated people the way I wanted to be treated (see Matthew 7:12). For example, I would go in early to work and prepare the coffee and make sure the conference room was in order. I would clean the kitchen area to help out the secretaries who were always busy. They appreciated that. I would make sure my supervisor's coffee cup was clean. I would pick up his *USA* newspaper every morning. I would make special arrangements when he and I would go to our favorite restaurant for lunch. One person once asked me (sarcastically) if I would even shine my boss's shoes if he told me to. I said, "Yes. Pride never pays your bills." That person hardly spoke to me after that. She was a bitter and unhappy person and had many problems at work. She ended up resigning one day and died shortly after that. I was stunned when I heard the news.

I did many things for the VA, and I helped many veterans. But the main thing I did was pray for our organization. On one hospital inspection, we got a 4.0. I remember praying fervently for that day because everyone in management was worried, and there was a lot of pressure on our employees. Even my supervisor asked me for advice weeks prior to the inspection. The result: we passed with flying colors. Why? Because I prayed. I wanted us to shine for once, and we did. And I am not bashful to say it was my prayers that helped make this happen. Maybe that's why I was spared as God watched over me in the Vietnam War.

Working for the VA is a unique challenge because you're dealing with veterans, people who have served their country, been to war, and are very sick. But it is also a rewarding experience. In the VA, you learn to appreciate your country a lot more. You become astutely aware of the price that was paid for your freedom. In fact, working for the VA made me more aware of myself as a veteran. It brought out the best of me.

However, things started to get bad. People were becoming extremely unhappy, and we had many problems in management. When I suggested to my supervisor and the director that we needed a pastoral service there at the VA to promote high morale and that I would be willing to do it as an extra duty, I was coldly denied. I was treated differently and then gradually banned from participating in any more special events. Things got so bad that we started losing staff. We lost our own secretary and really felt it (secretaries are the backbone of any office). Then I was told I would have to do more work. I was already overwhelmed. I hung in there until one day when I was called in by my supervisor. I was unjustly scolded because of a deadline that was missed, and I was accused of neglecting it. I was not aware of it, and it wasn't even my area of responsibility. That's was the straw that broke the camel's back. I got so upset that I got sick and ended up in the Support Team, which was, at the time, like an ER there at the VA. This was on October 2, 2006. Long story short, I retired almost immediately at the advice of my VA medical provider, who warned me about my health. In fact, I was retired exactly two weeks after that incident. I was placed on sick leave until I officially retired on October 16, 2006. Everything worked out in my favor. I retired on my own terms and at the grade I desired. It was another chapter in my life that came to an end but for a reason (Romans 8:28).

That same year, in November 2007, I heard things were getting unbearable at the VA. I was called at home by Channel 14, Fox Local News. They wanted to interview me because someone at the VA told them about me and was complaining desperately about the situation there. At first, I was upset and reluctant because I didn't need to get involved in any type of conflict, as I was still recuperating from my difficult departure. But I finally agreed, and they came to my home that afternoon. The interview took place outside on my front lawn. It was aired that night on KFOX TV News. The reporter asked me many questions, and I remember telling him that if things didn't change there at the VA, it would get worse. Well, they did. In February 2008, I read in the headlines of the *El Paso Times*, "El Paso VA: Worst in the Nation." Wow! What happened? I knew things were bad at the VA but worst in the nation? I was stunned. The three top management executives retired not too long after that. No elaboration needed here. By the way, two of them have passed since then.

What really happened? Very simple. First, they defied the Lord. Then they rejected a man of God. Who and what were these men? All I wanted was to do good, to edify, to make it better for everyone. The workplace does not have to be a battleground. But today, I keep hearing it's even worse. I know that they are critically short of staff, as I have seen the list of the many vacancies for doctors, nurses, and support personnel. And I myself have experienced the effects of this, such as having difficulty getting my meds on time, and a few of my appointments have been dubiously canceled. The problems apparently continue. But I dare not predict anything because I have learned to be fearful of my own prophecies. You see, a man of God can see things others can't. I actually saw this coming years ago, when things were becoming more complicated at the El Paso VA. I now see a similar pattern, and it is only a matter of … time.

I do not mean to sound critical of the VA, but if I am, it's because I care about it. You see, it is there where I go to get my care as a veteran and patient. It is there where I poured out my heart and worked so hard. It is there where I met some of the greatest people I've ever known. It is there where I learned to appreciate more my legacy as a war veteran. It is there where I managed to help many fellow veterans who were sick and desperate. And it is there where, in the privacy of my office one day, a father and his twenty-one-year-old son came to see me. The son had just returned from the Iraq War. The father was crying over his son, begging for help because his son was suffering severely from PTSD (post-traumatic stress disorder). As I looked at the young man, I noticed the glazed look in his eyes. Something was definitely wrong with this veteran, as he would not speak at all. I talked to them and prayed for them. Then I escorted them to the VBA (Veterans Benefits Administration) section of the VA. The good people at the VBA took it from there. I'll never forget that day. I'll never forget the tears on that father's face. And I'll certainly never forget how it affected me. It's a shame that because of the bureaucracy of the system, many who want to do good cannot. I tend to think maybe that's what's wrong with our country nowadays—that those who truly want to do what is good and what is right are for the most part ostracized. Despite all this, I am grateful for what I had to go through. I am grateful to the VA. For the man of God, there is a purpose for everything, good or bad. But my main point is that when a man of God is rejected at any level, bad things will happen to that person or organization.

> "For whoever is ashamed of Me and My words in this adulterous
> and sinful generation, of him the Son of Man also will be ashamed
> when He comes in the glory of His
> Father with holy angels."
> —Mark 8:38

> I dare not fall under this judgment.
> —(aah)

CHAPTER 9

PTSD

What Is PTSD?

P TSD is post-traumatic stress disorder. It is a form of anxiety disorder triggered by a traumatic experience that you lived through or witnessed.

The disorder may affect survivors of sexual assault, physical abuse, war, torture, natural disasters, automobile accidents, airplane crashes, hostage situations, or death camps. It can also affect rescue workers at an airplane crash or mass shooting or someone who witnessed a traumatic accident. Whatever the trauma, the person has lived through a period in which he or she was faced with intense fear, a sense of helplessness, and a loss of control.

People of all ages can have post-traumatic stress disorder. It's relatively common among adults. Post-traumatic stress disorder is especially common among those who have served in combat.

Post-traumatic stress disorder shares many of the same signs and symptoms of depression. The major difference is that with post-traumatic stress disorder, you continue to have prominent memories and intrusive thoughts of the event or events that initially triggered the disorder.

Signs and Symptoms

Signs and symptoms typically appear within months of the traumatic event. In some instances, they may not occur until many years later. There are thirteen specific symptoms or signs related to the disorder. These are:

1. Flashbacks, disturbing dreams, and hallucinations (very common among military combat veterans)
2. Shame or guilt
3. Upsetting dreams about the traumatic event
4. Trouble sleeping
5. Trying to avoid thinking or talking about the traumatic event
6. Irritability or anger (anger is a predominant sign in combat veterans)
7. Feeling emotionally numb
8. Poor relationships (failed marriages are common)
9. Hopelessness about the future
10. Trouble concentrating
11. Being easily startled or frightened (gunshots, explosions, etc.)
12. Hearing or seeing things that aren't there
13. Severe depression (the cause of many suicides)

Having post-traumatic stress disorder may also place you at a higher risk of other conditions such as drug abuse, alcohol abuse, and eating disorders.

Treatment

Treatment for PTSD often includes both medication and psychotherapy. The treatment depends on the type of disorder you have. With treatment, most people with anxiety disorders are able to resume everyday activities. For the most effective results, your doctor may recommend a combination of medication and psychotherapy.

Medications and Therapies

Several medications and therapies may relieve signs and symptoms of anxiety. These are:

Antidepressants. Many drugs used to treat depression also have anti-anxiety effects. In fact, antidepressants are the treatment of choice for some anxiety disorders. Examples of antidepressant drugs used to treat anxiety include fluoxetine (Prozac, Sarafem), paroxetine (Paxil, Brisdelle), and imipramine (Tofranil).

Anti-anxiety medications. Anti-anxiety medications include a class of tranquilizing drugs called benzodiazapines, as well as the medication buspirone (BuSpar, Vanspar).

Beta blockers. These medications work by blocking the stimulating effect of adrenaline (epinephrine). They may reduce heart rate, blood pressure, pounding of the heart, and shaking voice and limbs. Because of that, they may be used infrequently to control symptoms for a particular situation, such as giving a speech. They're not recommended for general treatment of anxiety disorder.

Psychotherapy. Types of psychotherapy that are especially effective in treating anxiety disorders are cognitive behavioral therapy, relaxation therapy, and desensitization and exposure therapy.

It is important to note that these do not work for everyone. Another important factor to be considered is side effects, which can sometimes be worse than the problem itself. The patient with PTSD will require constant care and attention. Post-traumatic stress disorder does not go away. Medication and therapy are only tools used to cope with this disorder. Follow-up care with a mental health professional is essential for the person with PTSD.

PTSD and War Veterans

For many war veterans, PTSD is a painful reality. Anyone who has experienced a terrible event may have PTSD. It is a psychiatric diagnosis given to those who have suffered life-threatening events in war, followed by severe traumatic thoughts related to the event or events.

Thousands of war veterans suffer from this disorder, trying to forget and to cope with this trauma. Many of these have turned to drugs or alcohol in order to cope with PTSD. They separate themselves from everything and everyone. You can sometimes see them in the streets, alone, confused, destitute, and sick. They've lost everything. They've lost their jobs, family, homes, and even their faith in God. These are the results of war. The person who has been in the front lines of battle, who has seen so much death and blood—that is, the horror of war—is never the same when they return. And as the years pass, this condition becomes worse. In many veterans, PTSD signs start within the first several months after the traumatic event. But the signs of PTSD can appear many years later. That's why it is called *post-traumatic*. Some veterans may get better in time, but the majority do not.

The classic signs of PTSD in war veterans are: anxiety, depression, nightmares, hallucinations, flashbacks, and extreme rage. In severe cases, ideation of suicide or homicide is common. Many veterans have taken their lives and the lives of others. Overall, PTSD affects all aspects of a person's life; it affects society. And although there is treatment for this disorder, very few, if any, recover from it.

Here is a personal testimonial from a Vietnam veteran with PTSD: "As a victim of that terrible war, I am filled with anger, anxiety, and fear. I have experienced severe depression and heavy substance abuse. Although I have tried not to think about what I have seen and been through, I still suffer those terrible nightmares and memories of war. PTSD has affected all aspects of my life. What has sustained me through all this has basically been my faith in God. Today, however, I have my VA benefits, and more importantly, a loving wife who understands me and comforts me with tender love and affection. I also still have my mother, whose prayers have always protected me from the adversities and dangers of life. I thank Almighty God for all this." That veteran is me. I wrote that years ago.

PTSD has been called the *silent killer* and the *hidden disease*. It's a mental health condition, one that you cannot see or get rid of or treat with a surgical knife. You can recover from a flesh wound. You cannot recover from a mental condition. This is a scientific fact. Recently, there was legislation submitted to Congress to approve a Purple Heart for combat veterans diagnosed with PTSD. It was disapproved. This is wrong. When you have this disorder, you are disabled. In many cases, if the condition is severe, you are unemployable. According to latest Veterans Administration (VA) statistics, there are twenty-two veterans committing suicide every day. About 75 percent of them have PTSD. That's about 495 a month.

The reality is that PTSD exists and affects millions of Americans. It is the result of all the tragedies and problems plaguing our country.

War, mass shootings in public places, terrorist attacks, and weather disasters are contributing factors that affect the human mind. These are the ramifications of our inability to live in peace and to do what is simply right. It is a heavy price our society is painfully paying, and make no mistake, we are paying for it, one way or another.

"What causes fights and quarrels among
you? Don't they come from your
desires that battle within you? You want something but don't get
it. You kill and covet, but you cannot have what you want.
You quarrel and fight."
—James 4:1–2 NKJV

There is a price for everything, especially war.
—(aah)

CHAPTER 10

War Veteran to Minister

A Spiritual Transformation

This part of the book deals with my spiritual transformation. That transformation is the reason for this book. Few people know or recognize me as an ordained minister, and even fewer as a theologian. I don't advertise this credential or title often. But I have been a student of the scriptures for many years since my spiritual conversion as a Christian. I have served in the various churches, Protestant and Catholic. I say "various" because they all differ in certain ways. I was officially ordained back in 1994 by a nondenominational Christian church that accepted my Profession of Faith.

I've served as a Sunday school teacher, a counselor, a deacon, and as an associate pastor. I've been through what I call "the religious mill." I call it that because of the different churches and their theologies. I've earned a master of arts in biblical studies and doctor of divinity degrees from bona fide and accredited schools. These had their price in more ways than one.

My main ministry was at the Border Immigration Detention Center Ministry here in El Paso. I was the minister and pastor there. To some I was even, yes, their priest! It was a thankless ministry in terms of lack of support and recognition. It was, in fact, a difficult and risky ministry. Very few dare to minister in such places. I ministered to men from countries like Mexico, Puerto Rico, Colombia, Guatemala, Cuba, Africa, Germany, Russia, Poland, Iraq, Afghanistan, and, yes, even Pakistan. One Sunday morning, to my great surprise, five Muslims attended my service. After hearing my sermon, one of them came forward and wanted to accept Christ. There were about 450 men there that day, the maximum that the hall room would hold. It's a day I'll never forget in my service to the Lord. Unfortunately, the other four Muslims did not agree with this, and the next Sunday, they did not show up because they had threatened the one Muslim's decision to become a Christian. I was later told by officials there that I was not to preach to people of the Muslim religion anymore. I told the officials it was not my place to ban anyone from the preaching of the Word of God. They didn't understand. It is the government and politics of our nation that are destroying us, not the Muslims. But that's a subject for another time.

I served in that ministry from 1993 to 2005. I was there every Sunday morning. It was a commitment I made in my service to the Lord. I believe I saved many souls; that is, I brought thousands of men to Christ. I performed many baptisms. In fact, men who left and returned to their homeland would write to me. One man from Africa started his own church and told me that my sermons inspired him to become a pastor. He kept writing to me, and his church had grown to about three hundred the last time I heard from him. He was a nice, humble man. There were other men who would write to me and tell me how their experience at the Detention Center changed their lives. In their letters, they asked me to pray for them and for advice. I'm talking about men who were hurting and desperate. They had families. They came from countries that were extremely poor and had practically no laws or civil rights. They were destitute, struggling for a better life. They came to our country searching for hope. It was heartbreaking to see such men … men who were just trying to make a living. I used to get home and cry over them. Sometimes I think maybe that's why I was spared in the Vietnam War. God had a divine plan for me. You never really know the lives you'll touch when you serve God. You never know where the ministry of the Lord will take you.

After 9/11, things got much more difficult at the Detention Center. Security measures got so bad that there were times I wasn't even allowed to enter the facility. Religious services would be canceled for the day. I had to present documentation verifying my status as a citizen. A complete investigation and high-security clearance was done on me. Of course, I passed. But then came that fateful day when I received a certified letter telling me that I was banned from giving any more services there because of my "preaching." I was preaching the Gospel. I was teaching the truth. I fought back with a stern letter to the director of the facility but to no avail. I had to accept the possibility that maybe God had closed that door for me, as things were getting dangerously ugly at the Detention Center. I had heard there were riots there and officers getting hurt. The men were questioning why wasn't I showing up, but this is what happens when they defy a man of God. Despite all this, I am reminded in Romans 8:28 that everything happens for a reason to those who love God. I've saved the souls that needed to be saved by me. I've done my duty. I had to let go and leave the rest to God. Yes, sometimes you just have to let go of those things you don't have control of and leave them to God Almighty. He will deal with them.

I don't know what the future holds, as things look really bleak these days. I just know that the end is very near. I say this because I know the scriptures, and I see the signs. The man of God sees things others can't. Those not in the Spirit are blind. Knowing all this, I pray every day. In fact, my wife and I pray at the dinner table every evening, giving thanks and praying for everyone and our country. The dinner table is our alter. I pray that God will have mercy on us all, because the truth is we're all sinners, no matter what and who we are. You see, prayer is the direct lifeline to God, because when you pray, He listens. We don't need all that religiosity, and it's not our church or our religion that saves us or makes us holy. It's the blood of Jesus Christ on that painful and bloody cross, where He died for our sins and our salvation. It's a love I'll never fully understand, and no one really does. But you know what? I believe it, and I accept it. It's the only real hope I have. This is what I tell people who I know need spiritual guidance. I tell it especially to some family members. They are very religious but don't really know the Lord. I say to them, "Did you know that you *can know* if you have eternal life?"

"These things I have written to you who believe in the name of the Son of God, that you may know that you have eternal life, and that you may continue to believe in the name of the Son of God." (1 John 5:13)

"And we know that the Son of God has come and has given us an understanding, that we may know Him who is true; and we are in Him who is true, in His Son Jesus Christ. This is the true God and eternal life." (1 John 5:20)

I cited these because there are many "religious" people out there who do not know their eternal fate. This is really sad, I think. Just one private and simple prayer can save a person's soul, by confessing their sin to God, in the name of Christ. It will change their life. You know why I'm still here, after war and all the adversities of life? Because of God. I give all the praise and glory to Him, for His mercy and blessing. On the Day of Judgment, I can only plead to Him to remember the good that I did in this world, in this life. That's all I can do, for I am only a sinner who believes in God.

Today, I'm retired and living as comfortably and as simply as I possibly can. My ministry is … myself. If I don't nurture my spiritual life and my body, what good am I to others? Then comes my wife. I am to love her as Christ loved the church. And finally, the godly principles I stand for. I minister wherever and whenever I can. I am free from all that legalism that religion throws at us. I don't like it. That way, I can walk into any church that invokes the name of our Lord Jesus Christ and worship with a free spirit.

Yes, from a war veteran to a minister, I have learned a lot and gone through a lot. I have realized the reason I'm still here. My own VA doctor recently told me I am here for a reason. She's read some of my writings. I have told people and the churches that I am a walking miracle. I am. How do you survive a war, in brutal combat, as a medic and come back without even a scratch?

Being a minister can be a rewarding experience. You touch people's lives, changing many. I have performed funerals and weddings, where you can actually preach the Word of God. It's the best time to reach people. And I will preach at any church that invites me. I've done that too. That's about all I can handle nowadays. You see, I've learned to realize my limitations. I do not want to end up like some men I've known who died before their time. And God knows I've seen many men die before their time. "Do not be foolish ... why should you die before your time?" (Ecclesiastes 7:17).

Who would have thought that someday I would be teaching and preaching the Word of God, especially after such a roller-coaster way of life? I sure didn't. But that's how God works. He calls you when He wants you. Your life is not your own. The apostle Paul was knocked to the ground by the Lord when he was called. His name was Saul before his conversion. He was a tax collector and persecuted Christians. But he became one of the Lord's most faithful and dedicated servants, establishing many churches and bringing thousands to Christ. Sometimes we have to be knocked down for God to get our attention. I know I have.

All I know is I was spared for a reason. I am a war veteran turned minister.

"But His word was in my heart like a burning fire shut up my bones; I was weary of holding it back, and I could not."
—Jeremiah 20:9 NKJV

A fighter fights, a preacher preaches, and a writer writes.
I'm all three of these.
—(aah)

CHAPTER 11

Religion or the Truth?

A Realistic Look at Religion

A re you religious? Have you ever really taken the time to profoundly study the scriptures (John 5:39)? Have you researched your religion or your church? Have you taken the time to examine their doctrine? For example, who says one must not eat meat on Fridays? Who says one must not marry? Who says we must go to church every Sunday? Who says one must do this and do that? Who? Certainly not God.

However, this is what we traditionally believe. When it pertains to church or religion, or what we think symbolizes God, we'll believe in what others tell us. But have we consciously endeavored to scrutinize the scriptures for ourselves to see what God really says? Have we taken the time to listen to God and hear what He is saying to us? No. The first ones we go to are the religionists, the ones who placed us in this state of ignorance and blindness in the first place, and who keep us in spiritual captivity; the ones who have inflicted us with that religious fear that torments the most profound part of our souls, that part that suffers and cries out for God's grace and forgiveness.

How absurd this whole thing is. It seems we have forgotten the reason our Lord Jesus Christ came into this world, to give us peace and security, a life of blessings and the abundance of things. But most of all, and more importantly, He came to give us that sacred salvation that many reject or know not how to receive. He came to remove that religious blindfold from our eyes so that we could see the light. "The light came into the world, but men loved the darkness more than the light" (John 3:19). How tragic it is that many will die eternally because of those who deceived us; that because of the doctrines of men, many are unable to reach the Savior, the one who suffered and died on that agonizing cross for the sins of all. Yes, how tragic this whole thing is!

The truth is that for many years most of us have been greatly deceived. We've been told "You can't do that. Don't do it that way. Do it this way. You have to do this." The most damaging one is "God doesn't need you." We suffer these things because we choose to believe them. We choose to believe those who have contaminated God's truth with their religious beliefs—things that have no biblical foundation and that have burdened us with so many demands when God simply says, "You experts in the law, woe to you, because you load people down with burdens they can hardly carry" (Luke 11:46). But the biggest seduction here is that to be approved by others, all we have to do is to *go along*. Agree with them, and you are accepted into their belief system. It is here where we become vulnerable to deceit and hurt. The deceit is subtle, and the hurt is painful. We become victims of spiritual abuse, which exists in all religions and practically all churches. That is why God judges the seven churches in Revelation, chapters 2–3. Which one is yours?

What, then, forms the basis of our beliefs? Is it our experience? Is it our knowledge? No. In most cases, we've chosen to accept someone else's decision—someone who came before us and presumably knows better. Very few of our daily decisions that are based on our actual knowledge are being made by us. This is especially true on important matters such as religion. In fact, the more religious the matter, the less likely we are to listen to our experience, and the readier we are to make someone else's ideas our own. Why? Because the heart needs to believe in something, and it believes in lies when it cannot find truth. That is why religion is so popular and powerful. And it doesn't matter what the belief system is, as long as it is firm, convenient, clear in its expectations of the follower, and rigid. Given these characteristics, we'll believe in almost anything or anyone. This is because the strangest behavior and belief can be, and has been, attributed to God. "It's God's way. It's the Word of God." Is it really? Are we certain of this?

For example, we go to our priests, rabbis, prophets, and ministers. They tell us to stop listening to ourselves. The worst of them will try to scare us away from ourselves—from what we oftentimes intuitively know. And we know. But we fall into that religious trap that subjects us to those who are sometimes worse sinners than we are. Yet when someone comes along with the truth, one who has experienced the realities of life, who has really suffered, who knows and understands more, and who has demonstrated with clear evidence of his spiritual conversion and life-changing experience that God demands of everyone, he is ostracized. He is mocked and disrespected, even by his own family. But let that apparently holy person come by, and many will bow and kiss his hand. Then they will go to their churches and do all those things that are contrary to scripture. They will sing with enthusiasm while their hearts are filled with greed, lust, and envy. Some of the meanest people I've known are Christians. Some of the cruelest men I've met are pastors. I'm neither one—that is, mean or cruel. What I do is from the heart.

Where is God in all this? In what condition is the heart? The soul? Who are we really worshipping, God or humanity? Who do we believe in, God or our religion? Of religion, there are many, but there is only one Christ. A lie is like a snowball; the more it goes around, the bigger it gets.

And that's how it is. The world and its religions are rigid in their hypocrisy. Many suffer poverty and depression, dominant ailments of the times, because they don't know the difference. Many wars have been caused by religion. People are blinded and captivated by their religion. They are slaves and prisoners of a world plagued with disease, evil, and deception. They live and die disgracefully. We live according to what we believe, and we die according to how we live.   That is why I am not a Catholic, a Baptist, a Pentecostal, a Methodist, or from any other religious group or denomination that humankind has created. I am free of all these. That is why I can walk into any church that invokes the name of the Lord and worships in fellowship, in the name of the Father, the Son, and the Holy Spirit. I am free because I have chosen the truth, and the truth is Jesus Christ. He is the one who died for my sins. I am forgiven because of Him. He, the Lord Jesus Christ, is the one I will have to face on the Day of Judgment. That is the day I truly fear. "I tell you, my friends, do not be afraid of those who kill the body and after that can do no more. But I will show you whom you should fear: Fear Him who, after the killing of the body, has power to throw you into hell. Yes, I tell you, fear Him" (Luke 12:4–5 NIV). The first time I saw this scripture in the Bible, it scared the hell out of me, literally. I've never been the same.

So if you talk to me about church and religion, be careful. I've been there, done that, and I can tell you that *all* are fallible. I've seen what religion does to people. The only thing worse than religion is war. Today, however, we are in a spiritual war. The children of God are in a war with the devil. Whether we like it or not, believe it or not, we're in a war against the evil forces of this world. If you don't believe this, just read the newspaper or watch TV. No elaboration needed here, unless you've been living as a hermit in a cave.

Doing good deeds is nice, but it's not enough. The churches are full of good deeds. They're full of those vociferous fools and clowns occupying the pulpits and demanding your money while they drive their nice cars and wear Rolex watches. And have you seen their homes? I have. What we need are soldiers of God. We need people who are not afraid to tell the truth. We need bold Christians who are not afraid to profess the Christ that we know and bring them to the feet of the Savior. Our religion means nothing if we can't bring souls to salvation. Remember that, if nothing else. Don't believe in salvation? Wait for my next book!

That should be our ministry and not all these religious practices and belief systems that mean nothing. Want to change the world? Then fight! Use what God has given you: yourself. It is easy preaching to the choir. Try preaching to the real world. Jesus did. It cost Him His life. But today, He sits at the right hand of the Father God (Acts 2:33). With Him will be all the believers in Him. That's where I want to be.

Religion or the truth? I've just told you.

"Pure and undefiled religion before God and the Father is this:
to visit orphans and widows in their trouble,
and to keep oneself unspotted from
the world."
—James 1:27 NKJV

He who speaks the truth is the truth.
—(aah)

CHAPTER 12

The Theology of the Antichrist

A Hypothetical Dialogue with God

I will now touch on a subject that most ministers of the Bible do not like or want to talk about and that the world does not believe in. It is a rather difficult and frightening one, and one that churchgoers do not like to hear about. But it is one of critical importance. Here is my way of expressing the subject. It is a spiritual message between me and God. It is based on scripture and the signs of the times. I urge you to read it.

Albert: There has been much speculation and theory about the coming of the Antichrist. This is a very scary area, and I would like to know what You can tell me about this because I believe many people are confused or just misinformed, including maybe myself.

God: As you say, this is a very scary area. Are you sure you want to go there?

Albert: Yes. I have to know. I've preached Your Word. I've served in the churches.

God: Okay. Brace yourself and listen very carefully. Jesus warned that the times of the Antichrist will be by far the worst the world has ever known. His discourse to the disciples regarding "the tribulation of those days" is recorded in Matthew, chapter 24, where He describes the signs of the end. The Antichrist will be a man who makes his debut upon the world stage with bold charm and charisma. Some of your theologians and Bible scholars believe he will come from the European Union or the Middle Eastern sectors. The scriptures are not really specific as to which country or nation he will come from, but they do suggest that he will emerge from a very powerful and corrupt nation. He will have tremendous influence on the people. He will be a man who has paid his dues in the military and the political sense, and many will follow him. He will enter the world stage with a reputation of being a powerful man of peace. Daniel 8:25 says that "Through his cunning … he shall destroy many." He will guarantee peace but in heart will wage more war (Daniel 9). Many thought, at the time, that Hitler was the Antichrist. Even your churches were teaching this. The problem with that theory was that the signs did not fit the times, and vice versa. Many of you thought President Obama was the Antichrist. Some of you still do.

Albert: I don't.

God: Yes, I know. The Antichrist will be a much more significant figure. He will be much more powerful and persuasive. He will literally hypnotize the world with his philosophy and will have a definite plan. The Antichrist's three-point plan for world denomination consists of: (1) a one-world economic system in which no one can buy or sell without a mark sanctioned by the Antichrist's administration; (2) a one-world government, now called the New World Order; and (3) a one-world religion that will eventually focus its worship on one religion. Under the Antichrist, the economy will be a cashless society in which every financial transaction can be electronically processed and monitored. This cashless society will be ostensibly presented to the world as a means to control drug lords, tax evaders, illegal immigrants, and "enemies" of the land. Sound familiar? It will be presented as a foolproof way to end theft or as the ultimate in convenience for the shopper who can go to the supermarket without even a wallet. Every financial transaction will be done by one simple plastic card. Sound familiar? Everything will be controlled by a super-hi-tech and sophisticated system called the internet. Sound familiar? People's needs will be totally determined by numbers, and the numbers will control everything and everyone. Sound familiar? To be more specific, the Antichrist will lie, rob, and destroy. You will be deceived, robbed, and even killed. And it doesn't matter who your political leaders will be; all these things and events will come to pass, whether you believe it or not.

Albert: Yes, I think I know all that, but can You explain why? I mean, what's causing all this? Why must all this happen?

God: Because it's your sin as a country to ignore Me. Today, the American media and the politicians would have you believe that everything is going to be all right and that the worst that can happen to America will be a temporary economic downfall. Wrong! While the exaltation of God in America has in the past brought you unparalleled blessings to your land, there is also no greater example of what happens to a people when I am ignored and banished from the fundamental principles of Christianity. That is why the Antichrist is coming. Many of you think he's already here. He's not. But the nations in their wickedness and ungodliness are ripe for such an event. The way is already being paved for this impending judgment. For example, in America today, just about everything goes. Every practice must be permitted, for you must not judge anyone. Every belief must be respected, for you must not be bigoted toward anyone. And every form of expression must be allowed, for you must not censor anyone. Sound familiar? You are under the illusion that you are free, but you are not. You are being held bondage to sin and your foolish religious beliefs. Read carefully from your Bible the following scripture. It is about your country:

> The Great Harlot who sits on the many waters ... Babylon the great. The mother of harlots and of the abominations of the earth ... the waters which you saw, where the harlot sits, are peoples, multitudes, nations, and tongues ... For all the nations have drunk of the wine of the wrath of

her fornication, the kings of the earth have committed fornication with her, and the merchants of the earth have become rich through the abundance of her luxury … therefore her plagues will come in one day---death and mourning and famine … and the merchants of the earth will weep and mourn over her, for no one buys their merchandise anymore … the merchants of these things, who became rich by her, will stand at a distance for FEAR of her torment, weeping and wailing … for in one hour such great riches came to nothing. (Revelation 17–18)

Did you get all that?

Albert: Yes, I think so, but can You elaborate a little? I'm somewhat confused.

God: Okay. The Great Harlot is described, and Babylon the Great is destroyed. But who is this harlot, and who is this great city or nation? Who is the Antichrist? One of your renowned preachers of a mega-size American church teaches that the Great Harlot is the Roman Catholic Church and that the pope is the Antichrist. That's a convenient concept for an anti-Catholic. Well, I don't care whether you're Catholic, Protestant, or any other type of religionist. Symbolically, America already fits this description. The Antichrist may very well come from within your own country. But here's more evidence as to the crux of My explanation. Read in your Bible again, and this time, try to read between the lines:

Has a nation changed its gods, which are not gods? But My people have changed their glory for what does not profit. Be astonished, O heavens, at this, and be horribly afraid; be very desolate, says the Lord. For My people have committed two evils: they have forsaken Me, the fountain of living waters, and hewn themselves cisterns—broken cisterns that can hold no water. (Jeremiah 2:11–13)

The truth is the nations have changed their gods. America has changed its true God: Me. You have replaced Me with your immoral laws and immoral lifestyles. Pretending to be wise, you have become fools. But only I know what is going to happen and when. You'll just have to go by the warning signs I've given you. How's this: You're driving down the road in a storm, and you see a sign that says Warning: Danger Ahead. Do you ignore it, or do you heed it? In the past, you've ignored the warning signs of war. You ignored the intentions of the Japanese Empire, and you got brutally attacked. You ignored the actions of the Third Reich; you paid a high price there too. You ignored the events of the Vietnam War; you disgracefully lost that war, a war that is still costing you. And you ignored the hate of radical Islam, and you were attacked right in your own backyard; 9/11 changed your lives. It changed your country. You still can't get over it. And today, you continue to ignore Me and find yourselves in a war against the devil himself. Political correctness, blatant corruption, and extreme immorality are the three main things that are plaguing your country, like a cancer that invades the body. Think about it. This is not complicated theology. Your American dream, as you like to call it, has become your American nightmare. You are sad and worried about the future. Many of you are panicking because of your unstable economy. You are saddened and brokenhearted by the killing of precious young children in their schools. Yes, I understand your pain. But don't worry; they are with Me now, enjoying heaven. But for you, it is a very bleak time right now for America. All of these are signs and labor pains of the impending end, yet you continue to ignore them. Is that enough for you, or do you want more?

Albert: No, no! I get the message. I don't think I need to know any more about this.

God: Good. Now leave it alone and just do My will. You'll be fine. Watch and pray.

Albert: One more thing, please, Lord. This is a lot of information. Can I share it with others?

God: Of course you can. Just remember, you may get some criticism. Not everyone believes this. Not everyone wants to hear it. Now go get some rest. You look exhausted.

The conversation ended with a long and deep silence. His message was terrifying. I mean it was terrifying! I thought, *Was it just me? Was it a dream, a delusion, or was it really God?* Then I figured it out. It was me. But wait! How could I come up with something like that? What moved me to write about a subject such as this one? Who dares to write about this person that's going to cause great pain and suffering? Why not talk about angels and maybe demons, something people understand better? Why talk about this … person? What kind of mind can produce such thoughts? I searched the scriptures for an applicable answer, and here is what I came up with:

The spiritual man makes judgments about all things,
but he himself is not subject to any man's judgment:
"For who has known the mind of the Lord that
He may instruct him?" But we have the
mind of Christ.
—1 Corinthians 2:15–16 NKJV

Those who believe in God, no explanation is necessary.
Those who do not believe in God, no explanation
is possible.
—St. Thomas Aquinas, theologian

CHAPTER 13

Freedom

An American Illusion

Is there a brave spirit among us? Can it be said what we really feel? Can we speak truth? I got up one morning thinking about freedom. I'm not sure exactly what triggered it, but maybe it's because I'm a war veteran who went to war with the ideology of protecting our country against the enemy known at that time called Communism. Maybe it's because of all the discouraging news I've been hearing and reading lately. Or maybe it's just because nothing good is happening in our country anymore. It seems everything is failing, like our freedom, more and more, each day.

What is freedom anyway? What does the word actually mean? *Webster's Dictionary* defines freedom as:

> The state or quality of being free; liberty; independence; exemption from arbitrary restrictions on a specified civil right; civil or political liberty; exemption or immunity from a specified obligation, discomfort; exemption or release from imprisonment; being able to act, move, use, etc. without hindrance or restraint; a being able of itself to choose or determine action freely; ease of movement or

performance; facility; a being free from the usual rules, patterns, etc.; a right or privilege.

That says it all, or does it? I must explain.

A lot of people in America believe they live in freedom, when in reality they live in a straitjacket. That's the term I heard used by a war veteran and Harvard law professor on CNN in his lecture about freedom. His view of freedom in this country was dim but realistic. It shook the audience he was talking to. The following are my views as an American citizen and war veteran. I have some things to say about our freedom.

It is often said that we live in a nation of laws. We have so many laws that even the authorities can't keep up with them, much less enforce them. As I said above, we go to war with the ideology of protecting our country. We send our troops to Godforsaken countries to fight for *their* freedom. Then we say, for *our* freedom. What freedom? Whose freedom? The minute you step out the door of your home, you are not free. You've got traffic signs all over telling you of the speed limit, like those ridiculous school zones of 15 mph. When was the last time you ran over a kid going over fifteen? Then you've got those public signs telling you that you can't drink and drive or you go to jail. Drinking and driving is a way of life in this country for many. It's a losing battle, like the war on drugs. You've got other things telling you that you can't do this and you can't do that. Don't eat this, don't drink that. And how about those red-light cameras at the intersections, watching you to see if you run a red light or make a complete stop? If a cop stops you, well, you'd better pray you don't get a ticket or go to jail, even if you know you didn't do anything illegal, because all the freedom in the world will not set you free that day.

What about that insane law in Arizona that authorizes cops to stop and detain you if you look suspicious, like an illegal immigrant? This too was on CNN. We did, however, allow that Pakistani guy to become an American citizen, the one who came close to blowing people up in Times Square. They claim this Arizona law may very well spread to states like Texas and New Mexico and others. What a concept! Actually, the concept is simple. If your skin color is less than white, watch out; they have the power and authority to arrest you (they call it "detain," but it really means "arrest"). You will have to prove your citizenship or show proper documentation, like a birth certificate or naturalization papers. How many of us carry these things? Of course, if you're white and a racist, you're for this law. But what if the cop is a Mexican American and a racist? What if he stops you, even though you're white and an American citizen, and he asks for proof of your citizenship, simply because you, or the vehicle you're driving, look "suspicious"? You never thought of that, did you? You can bet there'll be some of those. At the very least, they will make your life miserable for a while, because in this country, a cop can arrest you no matter what the evidence is, or lack of. The rule of law, innocent until proven guilty, is not absolute. You can be arrested at any time, for any reason, no matter how innocent you are. You will have to pay a fine or even get a lawyer to set you "free." How about your kids? Your kids can have you arrested if you spank them, because today it's called child abuse. A phone call by someone to Child Protective Services can land you in jail. The days of disciplining your child in the woodshed are long gone.

Your credit score now determines your quality of life. There are banks now that won't even accept you if your credit score does not meet their standards. Eventually, all banks, even credit unions, will require this.

Here's another example: if you live in an urban area, you are most likely being watched by hidden surveillance cameras watching every move you make. These cameras are everywhere. So be astute when you go to a mall, because if something happens and you're near the area where it happens, you become a suspect. And if you live out in the country, outside the city limits, where you think you're living comfortably and freely, you're fair game for anyone. Where are the cops then? Where's the freedom here? I could go on and on, like socialism and taxes. Is this the freedom I went to war for? Is this the freedom many died for? Is this the kind of freedom you desire?

So let's go back to the original question: what is freedom? What does it mean to be truly free? Let's ask a more profound question: what is the truth? And is there truth that can set us free? The Bible says, "And the truth shall set you free." In the spiritual sense, yes, this is true. But in the real world, a world inundated with laws, rules, and regulations, we are not really free. Only in the Lord are we truly free. This is because real freedom comes at a cost. Ultimately, Christ died so that we could be free from the curse of sin. That means we are free eternally. Thank God for that! But while here on earth, freedom cannot exist because of the sin of humankind. This is because it is humankind who destroys. It is humankind who goes to war. It is humankind who kills. It is humankind who is the real devil. It is humankind's law that imprisons us, deceiving us into thinking we are free. Just because a law is a law doesn't mean it's just or right. This is because humankind is imperfect, and our laws are imperfect.

I am not afraid of losing whatever freedom I have. What I am more afraid of is what I might have to do to keep it. I did not go to war, study hard, and work even harder for so many years just to have someone take my freedom away from me. I now truly understand what Patrick Henry meant when he said in his rousing speech to the Congress, "Give me liberty, or give me death." God gave us life and the freedom that comes with it. Who has the right to take it away from us?

Today, however, our government gives out free food, subsidized housing, free medical care, and free education to people from other countries. It allows just about anyone to become a citizen. Illegals come by the thousands seeking jobs and a better way of life. Our taxes pay for their free services, like small apartments housing up to five families. You wait for hours in an emergency room because there are illegals ahead of you. Your child's second-grade class is behind because over half of the class doesn't speak English. Cereals now come in a bilingual box to accommodate the non-English-speaking alien. You have to press one to hear your bank talk to you in English. People waving flags other than ours are squawking and screaming in the streets demanding rights and privileges they haven't earned. We call them immigrants or dreamers. Those who came here plotting to kill us, we call them terrorists. All of these have taken advantage of our freedom and turned it into a socialized nightmare. Their actions have robbed us of the freedoms we once had as Americans. But the worst of these woes is losing your job to someone from another country; that is, you've been fired because the company you work for wants to hire cheaper labor. Insult to injury, you've been told to train that person before you leave, if you want to collect pay. What happened here? You've been robbed of the freedom to protest against such injustice. The American worker has become the victim of a system that has taken their freedom and given it to an alien. It's happening in practically every city in America.

I ask again, is this freedom? The truth is freedom is an illusion. We are not truly free. But the biggest tragedy of this illusion is the loss of the precious blood that has been shed in vain over it. This is what boils my blood; this is what shakes my soul and mind. This is the reason I write—to educate everyone, to open those shut eyes of ignorance.

America's fighting men and women sacrifice much to ensure that our great nation stays free. We owe a debt of gratitude to the soldiers that have paid the ultimate price for this cause, as well as for those who are blessed enough to return from the battlefield, unscathed.
—Allen Boyd

Give me liberty or give me death!

"Now the Lord is the Spirit, and where the Spirit of the Lord is, there is freedom."
—2 Corinthians 3:17

We have the option to be free, not the freedom to be cowards.
—(aah)

CHAPTER 14

A Dialogue with the Enemy

A Psychological Perspective

Here's my perspective as to how the enemy we're fighting thinks. It's not that hard to figure out. You see, getting into the minds of others is like getting into their homes; you can see what's in there. We can do this if we really try. I wonder what it would be like to get into the mind of the enemy that we're fighting. I wonder what it's like to get into our own minds. What are the demons we struggle with? Who are they, really? Here's how I think the enemy thinks:

America: You attacked us on 9/11 because you hate us. We condemned your cowardly action against a country that will not tolerate your evil ways. We will prevail and defeat you in due time.

The Enemy: You are wrong. We are not cowards. What we did took strong courage because we knew we were going to die and face our maker. But we did not attack you simply because we hate you, as you erroneously imply. We attacked you because you are trying to impose your way of life on others. You are the ones who have troops all over the world and continue to wage war on countries that cannot defend themselves. Yet you still cannot win. You cannot win because it is *you* who are wrong. You are a wicked and spoiled people.

America: So you attack and kill innocent people?

The Enemy: Innocent? You are *not* innocent. You claim you are fighting for your freedom and to protect your people. But it is you who are evil and immoral. Your way of life is unholy. We attacked you because you are a threat to all of us who just want to live our lives according to our beliefs and faith. We are merely trying to defend ourselves from an immoral country that wages war. Your greed and pride is what is destroying you. Your American dream is nothing more than your arrogance and corruption to achieve those things that give you pleasure. Your churches and religions are immoral and corrupt. So who are you to judge us and our religion?

America: We are a Christian nation. The God of the Bible is our God. We will prevail against all enemies of this country.

The Enemy: Your forefathers were Christians and noble men, yes, but you are not. You have not won a war since the last world war, and you are not prevailing in today's wars. Your own president (Obama) has said you are not a Christian nation, that you are a nation of many religions and faiths. But in fact, you are a divided nation. Your government does not work. Your laws are worthless. You are nothing more than court jesters. We are not the enemy. You are your own enemy. It is you who are destroying yourselves, not us.

America: You're crazy. You people are insane. You kill yourselves to kill others. You murder your own people. You are evil.

The Enemy: Who's crazy? Who's insane? Who's evil? Your children commit suicide and murder. Your soldiers also commit suicide and kill each other. You kill your own babies before they are born and call it civil rights. Your schools are under attack by your very own. You favor the rich and neglect your poor and the old. Your women and children tell you what to do. Your men become women; your women become men. So, again, who's crazy? Who's insane? Who's the evil one?

America: We will eventually defeat you. We will win. We got Saddam and bin Laden. We'll get you too. You will *not* win this war.

The Enemy: Yes, you did get them, but it has changed nothing. It is you who are still at war, not us. Look at your airports. Look at your military. Look at your schools and even your churches. Just look at yourselves. You're scared. Paranoia and fear have plagued your country like a cancer that invades the body. You are sick and don't realize it. You've been defeated and do not know it. You're in denial because you are a proud and arrogant people. But you are blind and very wrong. Your war planes, your warships, and your nuclear arsenal, all those weapons of mass destruction mean nothing. You've lost your dignity and respect. The world is laughing at you. We're laughing at you. You call us insurgents. You call us terrorists. You are the insurgents! You are the terrorists! Look at the insurgency within yourselves. Look at how you terrorize your own people by taking their homes and violating their rights. Greed and the love of money is your way of life. That is why your god does not hear your prayers. You are the evil ones.

America: Enough of this nonsense! This discussion is finished!

The Enemy: Yes, it is.

The discussion is over. But in order to defeat our enemy, we must understand *why* they're our enemy. We must get into their minds. But first we must get into our own minds. We must look in the mirror and examine our souls. We must look at ourselves as we really are. We should not judge others until we judge ourselves. Our country, as great as it is, is far from being perfect. We must understand that. We must also understand that the enemy we are fighting was created by the same Creator: God. I have found that when I do this, I can prevail in every aspect of my personal life and have inner peace. I can deal with evil.

You see, a person, before their sin is forgiven, must first admit it and confess it. Until then, they are lost. It is the same with a nation. As a democracy, we think we are right because we've been taught that the majority rules. But that's false. Although the majority may win, the majority may not always be right. Past elections have proven this.

America is at a critical crossroads. Whichever road it chooses will determine its ultimate fate. Perhaps the best and simplest way to explain this theology is to consider the following scripture. Notice the principle behind it. It speaks for itself. It speaks to all of us. It's from the Word of our God:

> "Do not judge, or you too will be judged. For in the same way you
> judge others, you will be judged, and with same
> measure you use, it will be measured
> to you."
> —Matthew 7:1 NIV

> Have I gotten through to anyone?
> —(aah)

CHAPTER 15

Our Ailing Military

A Dangerous Dilemma

What has happened to our military? What's really going on? As a war veteran, I cannot believe what I am hearing, reading, and seeing. I am concerned for the lives of our current and future US military personnel. I want to honor those who have already served—that is, our veterans. As a veteran myself, I have some things to say to our nation and to all who love it. Our fate, other than in God, lies in our ability to protect this nation. For that, we need a strong and disciplined military. So here it goes. What you are about to read is politically incorrect but true. It is not for everyone; it is only for those who love and care about this country. It is for my brothers and sisters in arms.

I am appalled at what is becoming of our military. For eight years during the Obama administration, I watched on the news airways as hundreds of senior officers were forced to resign or retire because of their objections to the current policies wrecking the military. I watched and read about people who have never served a day in uniform showing great disrespect to the glorious traditions of the US military. I watched on the national news male ROTC cadets parading in red high heels, male soldiers conducting physical training wearing pregnancy simulators, combat units dealing with breastfeeding and lactation issues in the field, and sensitivity training becoming the standard operating procedure of the US military. I have seen and read about gays being openly accepted in our military. Naval ships have had to modify their trappings in order to accommodate women, a challenge still facing our navy. All this is simply disgusting.

I have watched and read about transgenders being authorized to serve in the ranks. Restrooms have been modified to accommodate these freaks. Yes, that's what they're called. I am only telling it the way it is. A man wanting to be a woman has become a popular thing in this country, like those coming out of the closet. Precedence has been given to women. For example, three females graduated from the US Army Ranger School under what I believe is the most dubious of circumstances. All this has happened because those in the high rankings of our military have chosen to look the other way and wash their hands of these egregious practices. They are more concerned about their careers than about the integrity and effectiveness of the American military. They have sold their souls to the devil. Yes, the devil! I say that with great care but with even greater conviction. Because when you go against the natural laws of God Almighty, you are inviting your doom. You are playing with fire.

But here's more. Here's the final nail in the coffin. On April 1, 2016, Secretary of Defense Ash Carter, with the full backing of the president, authorized the legal inclusion of women in the combat arms branches and special operations units of the United States armed forces. This is plain stupidity. It poses a great danger to the US military. Let me explain.

The evidence against women in direct combat from the Center for Military Readiness and the Marine Corps' $36 million, nine-month study and the performance of women at the Marine Infantry Officers Basic Course is overwhelming. Conclusive findings revealed that women are simply prone to more injuries than men, have less muscle mass, and do not have the upper body strength or the same aerobic lung capacity and aggressiveness to fulfill the military's combat readiness requirements and missions. These, gentlemen and ladies, are scientific facts. Yet the president, the secretary of defense, the secretary of the navy, and the secretary of the army refused to acknowledge that this scientific evidence exists.

But it does exist. It indicates that while women perform spectacularly in 80 percent of the jobs in the military (per DoD reports), the combat arms and special operations should be off limits, period! Women are simply inferior to men in terms of strength and endurance. This too is a scientific fact and not a discriminatory opinion.

The so-called experts often say that women have already served heroically in combat. This is true. But these are exceptions. They don't tell the whole story. A woman does not have the same temperament as a man, especially in the heat of combat—another scientific fact. There is a vast chasm between working in the rear or battalion station and on the battlefield. A 110-pound female cannot carry a 180-pound wounded male in a firefight, no matter how strong she may be. The laws of human strength do not permit it. I speak as a veteran combat medic.

Women serving in the combat arms and special forces is not just a bad idea but a horrific decision that puts this nation in mortal danger. Think about it. Would you like your nineteen-year-old daughter killed in action because of current policy? I don't think so. Unless of course you don't really care, and you are mainly interested in the $250,000 payment you will get from Uncle Sam for her death. Too graphic? Too cold? Well, I mentioned this because there are many who are content with such a benefit at the cost of their loved one. Yes, there are families like that.

Here's the thing. Returning fire during a military police security operation is not the same as being in all-out combat firefight. I should know. I was in some of those in Vietnam as a combat medic. Let me tell you, it's no place for a woman, I don't care how determined or qualified she may be. When it comes to combat, reality sets in. You will live or die.

The president and the secretary of defense are not dealing with reality. They have succumbed to this feminist fantasy based on false premises of gender neutrality. They see the world the way they want it to be, not the way it really is. Their policies are based on the illusion that genders are neutral and that none of this will affect the military's readiness. Wrong! There is no gender neutrality on the battlefield. In the battlefield, in combat, there is only death and suffering. Who wins is determined by who is standing last. That, ladies and gentlemen, is a fact.

The effect of all this is the escalation of terrorist attacks on our soil. Our enemies do not fear us. They see the weaknesses in our armed forces. They are more prepared for war than we are. I have seen actual films of their training and readiness. The North Korean soldiers are far better trained than our marines, I hate to say. They've been trained since childhood. Their intent is to ultimately kill Americans. Russian troops go through months of brutal boot camp training. A Russian troop coming out of boot camp is ready for war. He hungers for war. Even Iranian troops are better trained than our military. They're just itching for a war against us. They're waiting until our military becomes weaker. These three countries are just waiting for the right time. Then they will strike with full force. This is not just my opinion but the opinion of many (now retired) high-ranking military officers. They have warned our politicians about this. On a recent television documentary concerning boot camp training in the marines, it was shown how lax this training has become. Boot camp and basic training in our military is not what it used to be. According to what I saw in this report, drill instructors cannot curse or strike a recruit. They must be very careful how they treat recruits. Their stripes are on the line every day. The result: we're getting soft soldiers and marines. It is probably the main reason we're getting too many soldiers and marines with PTSD nowadays. Too many mama's boys in our military. I do not mean to offend anyone with this statement, but I had my ass kicked in navy boot camp and was called names I cannot print. I didn't like it, but it made me what I am today.

In today's war zones, troops can now contact their families by way of cell phones or the internet. In Vietnam, we were lucky to get month-old mail. Yes, there is a new breed of soldier today. He is not trained like he should be. He's been spoiled and nurtured. It is hurting the very core of the military. Discipline and guts are no longer the strength of our military. Professing to be strong, they've become weak.

Our military has but one mission: to wage war and annihilate the enemies of this nation. It must never be used as a social or political tool by naive and uninformed politicians and predatory lobbyists. The American citizen must be aware of these things. Your family, your job, and your freedom are at risk without a strong and moral military.

We have a relatively new president. We must alert him of these things as we see them. He will need our wisdom and advice about our nation's defense against our enemies. We must speak up, rise up. It's our nation, our country, our future, and our children's future that are at stake. Carl Von Clausewitz, the Prussian military philosopher, said, "War is a mere continuation of policy [politics] by other means." He was right. Our wars have become nothing but political tools, and our military is nothing more than a paper tiger. To deny this is to succumb to an ailing military that cries out for respect and admiration.

> If you faint in the day of adversity, your strength
> is weak.
> —Proverbs 24:10 NKJV

> We must never forget why we have, and why we need our military.
> Our armed forces exist solely to ensure our nation is safe,
> so that each and every one of us can sleep soundly
> at night, knowing we have guardians at the gate.
> —Allen West

CHAPTER 16

Woman

The Truth about Today's Woman

This is a topic that's difficult to talk about and one that few dare to broach. But it must be said. It is not meant to bash, trash, or demean women; quite the contrary. For it is the woman who is usually the rock of a home and marriage. It is the woman who bears children and suffers for them. It is the woman who carries the burden of a household. It is that efficient and bright female secretary who can make or break a company. It has been said that behind each great man, there is even a greater woman. This is true. Woman was created by God through the rib of a man (Adam's rib).

This is an area even preachers or ministers dare not touch. But how much clearer can scripture be (2 Timothy 12–14)? What is the principle here? The apostle Paul pulls no punches in 2 Timothy. Read your Bible. Don't have one? Get one. He clearly defines women's role in life, meaning women are subject to men, that they are under the authority of men. Just as Christ is the head of the church, a man is the head of his home. Period!

Some argue that this type of authority pertains only to the church. If you're a libertarian or a feminist, this is a convenient concept. But in a society that has deviated from the laws of God, this concept has become a way of life. Women have taken the role of authority over men in many of life's affairs. They have invaded all aspects of the workforce. They have entered the political arena holding high positions such as senators, congresswomen, and secretary of state. One woman almost became president. They have forced themselves into our military, causing it to lower its standards in order to accommodate their desires. They have taken over the household as breadwinners and authority over their husbands. The covenant of marriage has been broken under the no-fault divorce law, meaning a woman can divorce her husband at will. This law has fractured the structure of what a family should be. Today, most marriages end in divorce, mostly by women who have grown tired and bored of being married. It is no wonder our children are lost in drugs, alcohol, suicides, and crime. But probably the worst sin of them all is they have polluted the churches as pastors and ministers. Yes, polluted! Women were not called to be overseers of a church. This responsibility has been charged to men. And God is not a woman, as some female preachers have openly implied. Such teaching is extreme heresy and an abomination to the Lord. How stupid can they get!

In the United States, the role of women has changed dramatically. They've lost their identity as the weaker vessel, that of requiring the care and respect of men. Chivalry is almost nonexistent. The home, the family, has been destroyed by the modern woman who is not content and wants everything her way, and she wants it now. They call it women's rights or women's equality. What a crock of you-know-what. Our children have become victims of this modern-day woman. Watch the daily news, and you see and hear of teens killing each other, doing drugs, getting into trouble, and the mother weeping. But where's the father? He's nowhere to be found. He's gone. His wife divorced him. So she's having to work two, maybe three, jobs to pay the bills, leaving her children alone with no one to care for them or give them direction and discipline. She herself is tired, sick, and aging before their eyes. Oh, but wait! There's another problem. Don't dare discipline your child or you'll get arrested. Child Protective Services will be on your case before you know it.

Those countless shootings in Chicago, in which teens are killing each other every day, are the result of broken homes and destitute families. They've grown angry and desperate. Their blatant crimes are really a violent and frightened outcry for attention and help. They're lost in a cesspool of lawlessness and filth. How sad this whole thing is. And it's not only in Chicago; it's all over the nation. That teen in Texas who killed his parents did it because he was angry at them. His parents were divorced. His mother was living with another man. His father, too, had another woman. Get the picture here? The report was on CNN a few years ago.

The American family is falling apart at the seams. The lifestyles of the times have taken over the godly principles our nation was built upon. Homosexuality is now a way of life. Coming out of the closet is a popular thing nowadays. Gays are applauded when they come out. But it gets worse. Transgenders have now entered the arena of shame. Changes in public restrooms to accommodate them are in the works and mandated by laws. I repeat, men becoming women, women becoming men. This is sickening. Our country has gone insane. We are becoming more and more like Sodom and Gomorrah. Remember those two cities? God destroyed them in one day. There was extreme wailing and gnashing of the teeth. No elaboration needed here.

To deviate from the laws of God is to invite total ruin. No nation is exempt from God's judgment, no matter how big or powerful it may be. History has shown us that great empires have fallen when they ignore God. Our nation, because of its moral decay, is quickly heading in that direction. Political correctness has taken center stage. There is no dignity or integrity in politics. Satan's demons have taken a foothold on our nation's leaders. From the highest office to the lowliest entity, there is nothing but corruption and lies. They've sold their souls to the devil.

The fate of this country hinges on our lifestyle and our relationship with God. Are we a holy people or a pagan society? "'Be holy, for I am holy' saith the Lord" (1 Peter 1:16). God has called on His people. He is talking to us. Those natural disasters like the killer hurricanes and fires that are destroying the homes and lives of millions are not Mother Nature. They are God speaking to us. They are signs of an impending end. Seen the news lately? Our government is falling apart. Nothing but lies are coming out of Washington. Preachers on TV are preaching more and more about the end-times. This is scary even for me. All these are the result of the failing family, the destruction of the home, and the spiritual decay of the church ... "the pillar and foundation of the truth" (1 Timothy 3:15). What's happened to today's church? Where is the truth? Is there a brave spirit out there to tell it the way it is?

Now back to woman. Woman was created by God to accompany man, to be his bride and wife, to bear his children, and to raise the household. Not to be dominion over him or to nag him. If this should offend anyone, that's too bad. For "It is better to live in a corner of the roof than to share a house with a quarrelsome wife" (Proverbs 25:24). This one needs no explanation either.

At the writing of this book, there is another problem, one that is affecting our country severely. That sexually harassed woman. She's come out and wants justice to those who sexually abused her. They're coming out of the woodwork. How stupid can things get? These are women who wanted fame and fortune at any cost, and now, many years later, they're whining and complaining. But the worst part of this scenario is the men, those wimps that have succumbed to the whims of this insane craze. They're resigning from their professions because of these arrogant and selfish liars and losers. The only ones worse than these are the men who stand by those whiners and defend them. It's enough to make you puke, if you're a real man. One letter writer said a kick in the testosterone area or a slap in the face would have averted these sexual advances alleged by these … women. Men are now walking on eggshells hoping and praying no one accuses them of sexual abuse, because that's all it takes nowadays. One false allegation can ruin a man's entire career. Like I said, it's enough to make you puke. The modern-day woman has ruined her status as a gender becoming of respect and admiration. She has created a monster within her own being and has destroyed the good that man has to offer. She has lost her identity as a woman. She is, in fact, terrifying. It's truly a sad thing.

You know what really turns a man on? A woman who is clean and shuts her mouth. A woman who is strong and doesn't complain. A woman who can take a man's shit and gives it back to him. A woman who stands by him no matter what. That's all. They don't have to be today's wannabe's, just a woman.

My mother was a woman. Because of her, we had a family and a good home. She stuck it out with my dad, good times and bad times. She was content with what Dad could provide. She stayed home and took care of us. She was our doctor and nurse when we got sick. She was our counselor. She was strong. She was a woman of the times, when women were women and loving mothers. They're hard to find these days, real hard. I am the man I am today because of a … woman. My wife stays at home and takes care of me and our home. She's content and grateful. She doesn't have to be out there worrying about some predator or as part of some female conspiracy. She's a woman!

> "I do not permit a woman to teach or to have
> authority over a man; she must be silent.
> For Adam was formed first, then Eve. And
> Adam was not the one deceived;
> it was the woman who was deceived and became
> a sinner."
> —2 Timothy 12–14 NIV

> Women are the greatest things on earth; every man should
> own at least one!
> —(aah)

CHAPTER 17

Real Men

The Truth about Today's Men

Okay, guys, are you ready for this? Now shut up and read what I have to say to you. I've talked about women. Now I will talk about men. Yeah, you know, those muscle heads with beards and tattoos who think they look good and are God's gift to the universe. Well, here's a little message to the testosterone world. Can you handle the truth?

One upon a time, men wore the pants and wore them well. Women rarely had to open doors, and little old ladies never crossed the street alone. That's because men took charge. That's what they did. But somewhere along the way, the world decided it no longer needed men. Women's rights and law by law, men were stripped of their pants and left stranded on the road between boyhood and androgyny (androgyny means both male and female in one). But today, there are questions our genderless society has no answers for. The world sits idly by as cities and governments crumble. Children misbehave, and those little old ladies we once helped to cross the street remain on one side of the street for fear of the uncertain because there is now no one there to protect them. For the first time since bad guys, we need real heroes—I mean real heroes, not those wimps that have been labeled as heroes by a society duped by the politics of the times. You know what I'm talking about.

We need grown-ups. We need men to put down the plastic fork and pick up a steak knife. We need more men to step away from the salad bar and eat a real meal, like a steak cooked rare or a greasy burger and a twenty-ounce glass of beer. Don't listen to that medical pundit that tells you what to eat and what not to eat. You're going to die anyway. Eat and drink while you can because the day will come when you won't even be able to piss or take a shit.

We need men who'll speak out against a world full of corruption and complacency. We need men who will stop being sorry and instead just admit what they did and then move on. "Oh, I'm so sorry ..." Shut up, wimp! You haven't done anything that hasn't been done by everyone else. You're a man. Act like one! Don't let them judge you. Don't let them screw you over. That woman charging you of that stupid cliché, "sexual harassment," is a loser and a liar. She's no better or worse than you. Even Jesus said, "He who is without sin, cast the first stone ..." No one could challenge this, and they walked away. So what's your problem?

It's time for men to get their hands dirty and kick some ass. Yes, I said it, kick some ass! It's time to answer the call of manhood. Having kids doesn't make a man. Any fool can impregnate a woman and have brats. But a man, a real man, has only two things in life: his word and his balls, and he breaks them for no one.

We don't need a few good men. What we need is real men.

Then God said, "Let us make man in our image, in our
likeness, and let them rule over the fish of the sea and the
birds of the air, over the livestock, over all the earth,
and over all the creatures that move along the ground."
'Then man said, this is now bone of my
bones and flesh of my flesh;
she shall be called 'woman,'
for she was taken
out of man."
—Genesis 1:26, 2:23 NKJV

It's time for men to grow a pair!
—(aah)

CHAPTER 18

The American Dream

Another Illusion

On March 14, 2018, I turned seventy-two. As I look back on my life, I realize how fortunate and blessed I truly am. I think about all that has happened in my lifetime and what I have been through. It compels me to realize how fragile and temporary life is and to appreciate it more than ever before. It has made me reflect on all aspects of my life, from my childhood to the present, from a young boy to senior status, an age I never thought I'd reach. But then, that wasn't my call obviously. I'm still here, writing these words.

As I have said before, I was originally born in Mexico. I came to the United States of America with our mother when I was six years old. My biological father was killed shortly after I was born. He was a politician from a rich family, and he had many enemies. My mother wanted to come to America to give us a better life because, in those days, life for a widow in Mexico and with children was extremely hard. She wanted for us to live the American dream.

Allow me to elaborate. She remarried. She met my stepfather, Joel Hernandez, in El Paso, Texas. He was in the US Air Force. Like me, he was a veteran. He served as a line mechanic in WWII and Korea. To me, he was my dad. He knew what war is and what it does to a man. He was very strict and strong. When he said no, he meant no! I got only one whipping from him. That's all I needed because his whippings were brutal.

We lived in different states, Maine, Georgia, New York, and Louisiana. Each tour was an adventure for all of us because we got to meet different people and live in different cultures. The scenery was beautiful with lakes, rivers, forests, and waterfalls that would take your breath away. America is a beautiful country. But I also learned a lot. I learned what it means to be discriminated against. I learned to fight. I attended some of the best public schools in the country. In those days, teachers ruled, and the coaches kicked your ass if you got too out of line. Not only were we taught arithmetic, English, government, and history (the only subjects you really needed), but we were also taught to behave. There was a section in our report card that read "Deportment." You were graded in that area and in serious trouble if you flunked it. The worst thing you could do in those days was get caught smoking in the restroom or get into a fight, although a good ole fistfight settled things. And if there was a bully in the school, all you had to do was confront him, stand up to him, and maybe beat the crap out of him. No more bully. My dad taught us how to fight. He would not stand for sissies in his house. In fact, he told me, because I was the oldest, he didn't want to hear any whining out of me and that I was responsible for my brothers. Today's dads are wimps, I'm sorry to say.

Despite some problems in the family, I have been blessed with good parents. No family is perfect, but I feel I had a good childhood. In fact, I think I've just about experienced it all. Kindergarten. Cowboys and Indians. Elementary school. Middle school. BB guns and bikes. Little League baseball. Football. Basketball. Good old-fashioned fistfights. High school. Girlfriends. Rock and roll. The US Navy. Vietnam. War. Women. Sports cars (Firebirds and Trans Ams). Marriage. Divorce. More women. College. Bankruptcy. More college. Ministry. Health. Sickness. Career, success, and now happily married and retired. All this is part of the American dream. Some of it was fun and exciting. Some of it was pleasurable and rewarding. Some of it was hard and painful. Some of it was sad. But it was and is life. The hardest one was, of course, war. As a Vietnam War veteran, I know what war is, and it still haunts me. I don't care what people say or think; it's something that will be there for the rest of my life. But I've been blessed with the salvation from war. I came back. And as I marvel at my diplomas and my certificates on the walls of my study, I am stunned at my achievements. "My Lord, how did I do all this?" I ask myself.

God, country, and family in that order. I've had it all. But it all comes with a price. There is a price to pay for this dream. I strongly believe that. So as I see the world crumbling around me—and make no mistake, it is—I guess I can truly say I've lived the American dream, you know, that mythical dream that everyone pursues in this country. I call it mythical because not all can attain it, and not all will live it, despite all the glorified philosophy about it. The belief that you can be anything you want to be is a false hope. Not everyone can be a doctor or a lawyer or one of those glorified professions. It's what you make of what you've got that will get you your dream. Don't try to be something you're not meant to be. Be yourself. Be who you are. Dream realistically. It is much safer to be a realist than an optimist. Because whether we know it or not, our destiny has already been decided. Someone much higher has determined that. The following is an excerpt from the book *For My Country*.

> You see, without hard work and responsibility, there is no American Dream. Hard work lays the foundation. Our solidarity makes work pay—for all of us. For the greater good. That's what our vision of shared prosperity is all about. My dream is of a place and a time where America will once again be seen as the last best hope of earth. Only in America can someone start with nothing and achieve the American Dream. That's the greatness of this country. Part of the American Dream is to live long and die young. Only those Americans who are willing to die for their country are fit to live.

"And afterward, I will pour out my Spirit on all people. Your sons and daughters will prophesy, your old men will dream dreams, your young men will see visions."
—Joel 2:28 NKJV

Dream, dream, dream. Then ... wake up!
—(aah)

CHAPTER 19

Dems versus Reps

The Problem in Politics

This one is a no-brainer because we're dealing here with no-brainers! It is not meant to explain the science of American government but rather to point out how absurd this whole thing really is. You don't have to be a political scientist or strategist to understand the problems with our government.

The Republicans and Democrats, against each other, cannot accomplish anything. Our country is in chaos, and our government is in disarray. Both parties are behaving like spoiled stepchildren. Ask any one of them a question on the issues of the day, and all they give you is a verbal dissertation on … nothing. Or the usual excuse, "I can't comment on that."

Both parties claim to be the righteous ones. The Dems blame the Reps for everything gone bad, and vice versa. Who's right? Who's wrong? If you're pro-Democrat, the Dems are right. If you're pro-Republican, the Reps are right. No matter how wrong either one of these may be, you'll vote for your party of choice because you're pro this and pro that. You've been brainwashed. Americans have been fooled by fools.

All this reminds me of religion. The Protestant accuses the Catholic. The Catholic accuses the Protestant. A cousin of mine who is a priest in

Mexico says every group other than Catholics is a cult or a sect. A Baptist church I once attended and served in taught that the Catholic Church is the church of the devil. So, who's right and who's wrong? There are over 250 denominations in the United States, every one of them professing to be the true one.

Back to politics. Who's right? Who's wrong? What used to work thirty or forty years ago apparently doesn't work anymore. The right wing and the left wing don't work together anymore. Perhaps if we looked at the American eagle, our symbol of freedom and power, and applied the principle of its mighty flight, we could get past all this political calamity that's dividing our country. For example, if you look at the American eagle, it needs two wings to fly, a left and a right wing. We shouldn't get hung up about whether the right wing is operating at one time or the left wing is operating at another time. Both need to be working cooperatively and simultaneously for the eagle to fly mightily and effectively. The point is they must be in concert with each other if they are to be effective and the eagle is to fly mightily and effectively. The House and the Senate should learn from this simple concept.

Okay, Democrat or Republican? I am neither. I vote for the one who can convince me of his sincerity and prove to me his worth. He must be educated and hold a high degree of intelligence. I don't want morons governing my country. Above all, he must be a man of faith, faith in the true God of the Bible, a God-fearing man. Because without God, he can do nothing. Our founding fathers realized this. That's why we're the country that we are today. That's why we'd better get past all this political nonsense and stupidity if we are to survive as a nation.

Whatever our views are as Americans, we must always be cognizant of the government we have. No president, congress, or senate can function effectively without the checks and balances of our government. These checks and balances are comprised mainly of Democrats and Republicans. Without these, we are just another form of a dictatorship.

We condemn and judge other countries because of their governments. But are we really any better? We are, but only if our system of government works. It's not working. At the writing of this book, there looms the possibility of another government shutdown and nuclear war. How stupid is that? And why? Because they don't agree. It's the Dems versus the Reps.

Who wins? No one. Who loses? The people. When governments do not work, the people suffer.

The government shutdown of January 20, 2018, proved the incompetence of these two parties. It proved that we need a new system of government, that our political system is broken and is not working. I propose to get rid of the two parties. They're useless. They're nothing but obstacles. They are in fact destroying us. Each one has its own agenda with its own interests, and that's all they really care about. A president, a vice president, and a one-body Congress is all we really need. We don't need all those pork positions currently in place. Empower the Congress with the authority to impeach any president that gets out of line and change the two-thirds requirement to a simple 51 percent majority vote. Streamline the process to get this done. It's not that complicated. You know why it's complicated? Because they've made it complicated. They've made it complicated to justify their positions. The more complicated it is, the more confused you are. You're in no position to question or challenge it, much less understand it. That's the way they want it. Like the electoral college. How many Americans understand that system? They don't. See my point? When something doesn't work, you either fix it or replace it. Same with government.

The thing is the government of the United States of America has become too big and too complex and too costly. It needs a complete restructuring. That's what companies and corporations do when things aren't working. For example, we spend more money on our war machines than on anything else. Let me tell you all something. When a country spends more money on its military than on its people, its doom is imminent. When a government forgets its own, it is headed for destruction. You know why bad things are happening to countries like Mexico, where there are mass killings and extreme lawlessness? Because of a corrupt and callous government. The people have become victims of a political mob that shows no conscience or mercy. We are headed that way too, I dare say.

Right now, at the writing of this book, there is the high probability of a nuclear war with North Korea. In the state of Hawaii, there was a false drill of a nuclear attack by North Korea. At the time, people thought it was the real thing. They panicked. For over thirty hours, there was chaos in the streets. It was a scary thing to watch on the local news and on CNN. It showed the rest of us here in the States the disturbing reality that awaits us if nuclear war actually happens. And what is our government doing? Nothing. Instead, they are arguing about that ridiculous program called DACA (Deferred Action for Childhood Arrivals). They care more about those immigrants called dreamers than they do about the rights and safety of 327 million American citizens. All this is the result of lost priorities and bad government. It is the result of an inept system of government that is only getting worse each and every year.

There's insult to injury; politicians still get paid no matter what because it's written into law. That's enough to boil the blood of any hardworking, tax-paying American. Oh, and where's the president in all this? He's idle. He's doing nothing. He's but a puppet with shaky strings. He can lie to the world, bankrupt the nation, and start wars, but he can't save our government. All this is the result of the Dems versus Reps.

> "Moreover you shall select from all the people
> able men, such as fear God,
> men of truth, hating covetousness, and place such over them
> to be rulers of thousands, rulers of hundreds,
> rulers of fifties, and rulers of tens."
> —Exodus 18:21 NKJV

> Everything rises and falls on leadership.
> —Dr. John C. Maxwell

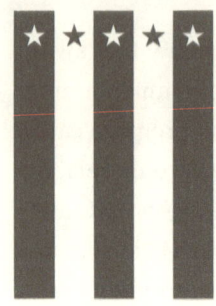

CHAPTER 20

Medicare, Social Security, and Taxes

A Letter to Congress and the President

I will now discuss a topic that affects every American citizen. It is one of crucial importance. I will be as brief as possible and to the point. Probably the best way to express my views on this subject is the following letter I wrote to Congress and the POTUS:

> As I listen to the national news CNN, MSNBC, 60-Minutes, Meet the Press, Face the Nation, and other media concerning Social Security and Medicare, I am stunned that there are proposals to cut Medicare and Social Security benefits in order to "balance the budget." Here are my views concerning how the proposed cuts will effect the livelihood of seniors and veterans, and our country as a whole:

I paid Social Security taxes since I was 19 years old. I'm 71 now, a disabled Vietnam War veteran, and retired federal employee of 36 years. My Social Security payments, and those of millions of other Americans, were safely invested in an interest bearing account for decades until Washington decided to raid the account and use our money for political initiatives, thus bankrupting (according to government economists) the Social Security System. Now, members of Congress want to raise the retirement age up to 70 so that by that time many of us will get very sick and just die. This is disgraceful and immoral on the part of our government.

Every day about 48 million seniors count on Medicare for lifesaving medications, doctor visits, and hospital care. Fifty-plus million seniors receive Social Security, and for most it is their main source of income. They're actually living at the poverty level. The guarantee of Medicare ensures that seniors receive the medical care they are entitled to. Medicare is a promise that was made to all Americans. Before Medicare was created, only a small percentage of Americans older than 65 had some kind of health coverage but private insurers were terminating coverage to those in the greatest need of care. Our nation knew that. It knew that it had to do better than that for its seniors and its veterans. You cannot balance the budget on the backs of America's seniors and veterans. This nation was built and defended by them. Please remember that the next time you think about cutting Medicare and Social Security on seniors and veterans. Remember also that someday, your children and grandchildren, will need such programs. They'll need that program and benefit that will take care of them. Now, for those who are not entitled to these programs, then they simply don't deserve them. That's why Medicaid was created. ON THIS NOTE: Incoming immigrants and refugees should not be getting Medicare or Social Security benefits. They should be required to meet the same requirements as Americans. Citizenship should be the first requirement.

In one of his State of the Union messages, the previous President, Obama, promised NOT to "slash" Social Security. Furthermore, experts on Social Security state that the program has ways to keep its funds flowing. The program has a "trust fund" that was built up during the surplus years, which has allowed it to pay beneficiaries in full until at least the year 2036. Even after that, the program's expected payroll-tax revenue would allow it to pay reduced benefits. So what's the problem? Are you robbing from it to fund other "initiatives" like futile wars and financial aid to other countries? That's not just my opinion, but the perception of millions of Americans.

I, and millions of other Americans, have been paying into Medicare from Day One, and now Congress wants to cut that too? Again, I, and millions of other Americans, have been paying income taxes our entire lives. Those in our government who want to cut our Medicare and Social Security benefits do not seem to realize the serious ramifications that could arise. People will become desperate. Many will commit suicide. Some will just die. Others will resort to violent protests. There will be chaos in our country like never before.

If you don't believe this can happen, then please let me remind you of all the protesting going on right now. What has happened in other countries where protests lead to extreme violence can happen here too. There could be complete chaos in this country, a chaos that could totally crush the social and economic status of our country, as we know it today. It could get so bad that those in Washington would have to run for the hills. When the people of a nation get desperate and angry enough, no politician or ruler can stop them. This is not just an opinion or a myth; it is a FACT! I personally have heard some heated discussions from angry people concerning this issue, and let me tell you, it's not pretty. To tell you the truth, it worries me. I would hate to see that happen in my city, in my country, the United States of America, the country I love and went to war for (Vietnam). Haven't we learned from the tragedies caused by anger?

Cutting Social Security and Medicare is NOT the answer to solving the debt crisis. It never has been, and never will be. It is the reckless spending by the Congress that is the problem. To tell us that our Medicare and Social Security benefits may suffer in order to balance the budget or to reduce the deficit, is WRONG and IMMORAL! It is vehemently unacceptable and will NOT work. Americans will no longer tolerate such dysfunctional performance by our elected representatives. STOP those costly political wars. STOP giving billions to other countries. STOP giving benefits to all immigrants that come here illegally, and to those who refuse to become American citizens and defend our country. And, STOP the "alien" that comes here to kill Americans! Then, and only then, can you balance the budget. It's Economics and Government 101.

As an American citizen, a senior, a war veteran, and as an active voter,

I urge the Congress and the President of the United States of America, to reconsider any intent or "compromise" on cutting Medicare and Social Security. We have a new Administration, a new President. We, The American People, now expect results. The fate of this country rests on how we take care of our own. Remember this, we voted you in, we can vote you out.

That was my letter to Washington. It caused attention. Both the POTUS and my congressman replied, assuring me that these benefits and entitlements would not be affected. If they hear it from enough of us, they'll get the message.

> "For our struggle is not against flesh and blood, but
> against the rulers, against the authorities, against the
> powers of this dark world and against the
> spiritual forces of evil in the heavenly realms."
> —Ephesians 6:12 NKJV

Never be afraid to defend what is yours, or you'll lose it.
—(aah)

CHAPTER 21

Euthanasia

Moral and Legal Issues

This is a sensitive and extremely difficult subject too often ignored by society, one that affects almost every American family and causes needless pain and suffering.

First, I must define euthanasia. It is important to understand what we are actually talking about. Euthanasia, in the legal sense, is "The act or practice of painlessly putting to death persons suffering from incurable and distressing disease as an act of mercy" (*Black's Law Dictionary*).

In the debate surrounding euthanasia, there are two distinct concepts that have evolved: *passive* and *active* euthanasia. I do not believe there is any relevant moral difference between the two. Passive euthanasia is the bringing about of death by not doing something, such as not continuing medical treatment. Thus the person is not killed by direct action but by deliberate neglect. In contrast, active euthanasia means directly killing an individual in order to eliminate further suffering. Active euthanasia is also called "mercy killing" since the motivation appears to be compassion toward the suffering patient.

But in both cases, the intent is to bring closure to suffering by death. Is there really a difference between withholding medical treatment in order to bring about death and giving a lethal injection? The law implies that there is. Therefore, euthanasia can be defined and classified as *withholding or withdrawing treatment for the purpose of bringing about or hastening death, or taking specific, deliberate steps to end a life when that person is not imminently dying.*

In a world full of people's rights, euthanasia has its philosophical viewpoints of the right to die. The belief that every individual has the right to control their own life extends to their right to end it. In its modern form, the right to die means the right to death upon request or demand. In former days, the right to die merely meant the right to die a natural death, without burdensome medical care. But today, dying is not without medico/legal implications. Unless one does not care, planning for death is now almost a requirement. It seems that you simply cannot die nowadays, at least not without affecting the livelihood of others. And if that's not enough, consider the cost to bury someone. These are factors to be considered.

In this age of cardiopulmonary resuscitation, ventilators, and other sophisticated means of life support, the prospect of over treatment, of being kept alive artificially, presents the average person with the possibility of experiencing a life they neither desire nor enjoy. Therefore, the right to die is asserted, whereby resuscitation and life support can be withheld. The desire to die of natural causes rather than prolonging the process by technology is what most people mean when they talk about the right to die.

Here's an interesting point: if a right to death upon demand does exist, one's health or life expectancy has little to do with the decision. Even a healthy individual would have the right to take their own life should life become intolerable. But does this gives us the right to die? Are we really free to make this choice? Well, let's examine the legal and moral principles on this matter.

This section is not intended to cite or explain the law concerning euthanasia but rather to present some principles the laws are derived from.

The principle of autonomy projects a person as a competent decision maker, capable of determining what is or not in their own best interest. The term "autonomy" means "self-rule." It has become synonymous with the right of individuals to choose for themselves, to enjoy personal privacy, and to assume personal responsibility.

American culture reveres the notion of individual autonomy, as evidenced by our Bill of Rights. Personal freedom is also consecrated in the US Constitution. Our autonomy and freedom are legal because of these two documents.

In medicine, however, respect for a patient's autonomy drives our belief that an individual should be asked for his or her consent before medical treatment is provided. People have the right to be informed of their physical condition, what treatments are available, and the risks of proposed treatments. These rights are protected by law. Once informed, the individual has the right to grant or refuse consent for a particular treatment, since they know their own self-interest best. Informed consent assumes that a person has the capacity to understand the information they receive and the ability to give voluntary consent. From a legal standpoint, it means that they have reached legal adulthood, and the law considers them to be a competent decision maker. When a patient is not a legal adult, a parent or guardian possessing mental competency must provide consent. This is standard procedure.

Competency is also an issue in informed consent since many legal adults lack the mental or physical ability to participate in decision-making. An unconscious or mentally impaired person is unable to comprehend the facts or make an informed decision. It is here where the crux of many problems lies in the practice of medicine, especially when dealing with euthanasia.

I now want to discuss non-maleficence. The principle of non-maleficence precludes physicians from harming their patients, better known as "first do no harm" (primum non nocere). The Hippocratic oath recognizes that a physician's foremost duty is to avoid harming the patient. Non-maleficence figures prominently in medical malpractice lawsuits, since modern tort law involves such matters as negligence, personal injury, and compensation. When a physician injures a patient through negligence or malice (maleficence), they have breached their obligation to avoid harm. The failure to conduct a medical exam that would have revealed a threat to a patient's health is as much a breach of this ethic as performing unnecessary surgery. When a patient with AIDS asks their physician not to reveal the diagnosis to others, does the physician harm the patient by telling the family? Or is the family harmed by not being told? When a patient is dying of terminal cancer and is suffering, which harm is greater, telling or not telling the family? Which one constitutes harm? Both. But it has to be done.

Tragically, physicians are sued today if they are unwilling to conduct exams that might reveal a defective unborn child. Public morality has changed to such a degree that the courts now award large monetary judgments to people whose children are born with handicaps. The result is that those physicians who are unwilling to conduct search and destroy missions on unborn patients are punished.

The difference between "killing" and "letting die" is another area where the principle of non-maleficence applies. When a patient is in extreme pain, does the physician have a duty to kill the patient, especially when the patient is unable to ask the physician to do so? Is the principle of non-maleficence violated by a physician's withholding or withdrawing a treatment with the intent to hasten death? Is there justice in this principle? How do we determine justice?

Our concept of justice arises from a notion of fairness. Fairness is important in our culture, given the urgency with which most people assert individual rights. Most believe one should shoulder more than their share of burdens. In an ideal world, everyone shoulders an equal weight. However, we do not live in an ideal world. So whose sense of justice should we use? When there are competing claims for the last bed in an intensive care unit or for the remaining kidney dialysis machine, who decides which patient receives care and which one does not? Should the person with the ability to pay preempt the one with limited financial resources? Should social standing be a valid criterion? The truth is that even in the medical field, justice is too often determined by money, power, race, or a combination of all. That's the world we live in; that's reality.

I will now deal with the moral aspect of this subject. This, in my opinion, is the more difficult part of the subject because it deals with principles few dare to explore. Although I've called it moral, I'm really talking about biblical principles. In truth, our morals are derived from the Word of God—that is, the Bible.

I've spoken about the right to die, and I've presented some legal aspects or principles concerning euthanasia, and although "the right to die" concept has its philosophical merits, there are several biblical arguments to be made against the claim for this right. First, God is sovereign, and He alone determines the length of days (1 Samuel 2:6; Psalm 39:4). Second, a Christian does not own him/herself, for we have all been purchased with a price by God (1 Corinthians 6:19b–20). Since we do not own ourselves, we have no right to dispose of ourselves. God determines when, where, and under what circumstances our lives will come to an end. Third, to consider the right to die as an inalienable right enjoyed under the Constitution means that it should be self-evident and derived from a law higher than humankind's. How, then, do we explain Christianity's significant influence upon cultures, causing them to allow suicide, murder, and mercy killing? Assisted suicide has been considered a criminal offense for centuries. If anything is self-evident, it is that murder, including self-murder, is wrong. Fourth, physical life is intrinsically good, not merely a means to another good. Our bodies are not incidental to our existence; they are an integral aspect of our being. If the body were not significant to being but merely "the tomb of the souls," as Plato described it, why would God bother to resurrect and glorify it? Why not just create an entirely new body or create beings with no body at all?

Since the body is important to our being and because bodily life is good, it is improper to speak of continued bodily life as a burden. If physical life is not inherently good, and if "to live is Christ, and to die is gain" (Philippians 1:21), why do we attempt to extend this earthly life? Why would any Christian go to a doctor? If the body is insignificant, why spend so much time and money trying to keep it healthy and why spend billions on health care? We may not understand the purpose of our bodily existence on earth, but that does not mean there is no purpose. We may not desire to live a life devoid of quality, but the notion of quality of life is subjective and arbitrary. Few would desire a life sustained by locusts and honey, with sackcloth for dress, and a home in the wilderness, but shouldn't we be grateful that John the Baptist lived such a life? One of the consequences of belief in the sovereignty of God is accepting the fact He often chooses to do things differently than we would. Sometimes that may mean an earthly life characterized by deprivation and hardship. But because of our concept of "quality of life," we as Americans generally cannot accept these conditions, and therefore we strive to prolong life according to our standards and expectations. But this is sometimes very wrong.

On the other hand, the right to die may be legitimate if it means the right to refuse burdensome and costly medical treatment when terminally ill, if such treatment is of little or no benefit. Traditional principles of medical ethics and the law recognize patient autonomy, which includes the right to refuse treatment. Very interestingly though, I need to say that individual autonomy is not entirely outside the biblical framework of humankind. I must explain: Within the Christian theology, we have a degree of autonomy in that we are divine image bearers, meaning we are rational, thinking beings to whom God grants the power to make certain decisions. In fact, decision-making is one of our most human traits. Everything we do, whether right or wrong, is based on decision. But! Our autonomy to make decisions is never without a price and does not exclude us from our responsibilities. That is, we have the freedom to make our choices, but we are never free to escape the consequences. This is something we should teach our teenagers.

Inevitably, the issue is who has ultimate control over individual lives. We must be careful to remember that the ultimate claim to our lives belongs not to ourselves or the state but to God. Asserting the right to die is the logical extension of humanism, which basically holds that humankind is the center of all things. We are not. God is. However, when we consider all of the control humankind assumes over the entrance gates of life, it should come to no surprise that humankind will seek to extend that control beyond its authority. This is where we falter miserably sometimes.

The above information has been based on intense study, knowledge, and personal experience. I will now present my personal feelings concerning the subject of euthanasia.

For the child of God, death means a departure from earthly life and entrance into the presence of God for eternity (see 2 Corinthians 5:1–10). To be absent from the physical body is to be present with the Lord, the greatest hope of every believer. "Precious in the sight of the Lord is the death of His godly ones" (Psalm 116:15). Notice it says, "of His godly ones." Proverbs 8:36 says, "All those who hate me (God) love death." How is death portrayed in modern culture? Popular music is filled with references to it. Many songs glorify death. It is no wonder that suicide is a leading cause of death nowadays among teenagers, reaching epidemic proportions. Television portrays death as a take it or leave it issue. Death is not an issue. It is a reality. It is a reality that everyone will someday have to face, regardless of our personal beliefs. I saw this reality when I witnessed my younger brother's agonistic suffering in his last days, due to cancer. He died of stomach cancer, a very painful and dreadful disease. I saw a fifty-six-year-old man turn into a sickly one-hundred-year-old-looking (or older) man within just a few weeks. In his last days, his suffering consisted of unbearable pain with the only treatment being high doses of intravenous morphine. Then it got even worse, until the end. It was then when I developed a whole new perspective on life and death. Given this painful and shocking experience, the concept of euthanasia does not appear now so inhumane or ungodly to me. Seeing my brother die like that affected me more than I can explain. No one should be left to suffer so much just to please others' traditions and beliefs. I'm literally sick and tired of that, and you should be too, if you have experienced the painful death of a loved one.

So let me spare you the pain of seeing a loved one suffering and dying. I fearfully believe that, under special and justifiable circumstances, euthanasia should be applied to humans. But it must be done with a sincere conscience and fervent prayer under the fear of God. There is no need for prolonged and painful suffering of the dying. It's, in a way, inhumane and selfish. Let them go. They want to die.

Consider this concept. When you are not feeling good and you're in constant pain, what do you do? You go see a doctor. You don't want to keep suffering. You will do what the doctor tells you to and take whatever medication they give you. If it is pain pills, you will take them. You will do what's necessary to alleviate the pain. This is what euthanasia basically is, alleviating the suffering. No one likes to suffer. No one. In cases of terminal illness with unbearable pain, the option is obvious. Kevorkian had the right idea. His problem was the crude way he went about it. But we are not Kevorkians. We are intelligent and compassionate beings. We must take the proper steps to alleviate the suffering of the dying. Death is inevitable, but extreme pain and suffering does not have to be. That's the point I'm trying to make.

It is always amazing to me that we can put innocent animals "to sleep" because we cannot see them suffer, yet we allow humans to undergo needless suffering and pain, knowing full well the expected outcome.

Somehow, this just doesn't seem right. So! Don't let this happen to you. Tell your loved ones, or those who need to know, your intentions for when that fatal hour arrives. Don't suffer any more than you have to. Resign yourself to the facts and get right with your Maker. That's all you have to do.

"What is your life? You are a mist that appears for a little while
and then vanishes."
—James 4:14

There are only two things I really fear in life: God and some
damn disease that creeps up on you and then
kills you.
—(aah)

CHAPTER 22

The Flag and the
National Anthem

A Freedom of Speech Dilemma

This is a sensitive and complicated subject that is too often taken out of context. It is one that is misused in the interest of personal gain and one that is affecting the spirit of this great nation.

The recent publicity of NFL athletes refusing to stand for the national anthem and show respect for the flag, and a president who called them SOBs, ignited national outrage that dominated the news on practically every TV station.

As a war veteran, I was appalled. I could not believe what I was seeing and hearing. The disrespect by these athletes and the deplorable deportment of politicians is something I never thought I'd see in my day. But I did.

Some will argue that it's about freedom of speech, that we have the right to express what we want for any cause. That's true, but we should use this right in a more decent and respectable manner. The standing for the national anthem and the flag before a sports game is a special and solemn moment. It should be respected and honored by *everyone* in attendance.

Leave your protesting for an appropriate time and place. The freedom of speech right was created by our founding fathers so that we, as a people, would not have to suffer suppression by dictators or any authoritarian type of government. It was incorporated in the Constitution under the First Amendment to ensure that every American has the right to petition the government of the nation without retaliation from that government. This freedom of speech right was never meant or designed to defame our country in any way, shape, or form and for any reason.

The flag and the national anthem are symbolic expressions of our identity as Americans. They are, in fact, a fervent and spiritual outcry of our desire to be free. Too many gave their lives for the very freedoms that we enjoy today. Too much blood was shed for these freedoms. It is disgusting to see a professional athlete behave in such a manner. But what is more disgusting is those who are in leadership positions openly allowing such behavior.

Is it too much to ask those who need to protest to allow a few minutes for the presentation of the flag and the national anthem? Is it too much to ask for respect for those who served to protect the very freedoms these arrogant athletes take for granted? Is it?

While we live in a free society and are free to speak our minds, we are never free to defy that which is ordained by God. Our country was ordained by God because of the God-fearing men who formed it. To defy that which is ordained by God is to invite internal doom. I pray that our nation wakes up and realizes the severity of this unfortunate matter. The freedom of speech is a sacred right. It is only viable and effective when we use it wisely and conscientiously.

"Let my accusers be clothed with shame, and let them cover
themselves with their own disgrace as with
a mantle."
—Psalm 109:29 NKJV

God, country, and family. In that order.
—(aah)

CHAPTER 23

Mass School Shootings

Our Nation under Attack from Within

The mass school shooting at Marjory Stoneman Douglas High School in Parkland, Florida, on February 16, 2018, is an indication that we are under attack from within and from our very own. At the writing of this book, there was another one in Santa Fe, Texas, on Friday, May 18, 2018. Ten killed, and ten wounded. Eight of the ten were students, and two were teachers. Per CNN reports, there have been at least twenty-three school shootings this year in the United States, almost one per week. The claim is that in these shootings, there have been more fatalities than in the wars of Iraq and Afghanistan combined.

These shootings have shaken our country to the point where we are now living under the cloud of fear. It is a topic that needs to be discussed, with decisive action taken. We no longer have the luxury of ignoring the subject. It is a problem that is going to change the way our kids go to our schools. It will affect you and me also. These shootings alone have changed our country, driving us into a paranoiac state of mind and division. If you are the parent of a young child or a teen still in school, you are fair game for the heartache and horror that may follow by some angry perpetrator out there planning the next attack on your kids. This is a reality that has hit every American family right in the face.

But let's not mix up our words and philosophies. If it was the terrorists shooting up our classrooms, we would have already launched a reckless attack overseas in retaliation. Remember how stupidly we reacted after 9/11? We bombed the hell out of a country that was not the one at fault and ended up in a frivolous war that is still going on, costing us billions and more lives.

But these attacks are from within. At an appalling and quickening pace, growing numbers of Americans are being massacred at churches, concerts, nightclubs, shopping malls, and classrooms. We are doing virtually nothing to stop the slaughter.

Tragically, images of traumatized students, rushing in single file out of classrooms with their hands in the air under the protective muzzles of police rifles, have become all too familiar. It's a disturbing scene.

The feeble responses of leaders, political and social, with sayings like "It's absolutely pure evil," "It's a mental health problem," and the most hypocritical one, "Our thoughts and prayers are with you" are just that, feeble. Not a mention of the weapons being used to carry out these massacres is heard. No real plans to deal with this crisis.

The argument right now is whether to separate the most disturbed individuals from the deadliest weapons. It's an argument that has no solution. It is not the mental health condition of these shooters that is the problem. It's us. Yes, us! Let me explain. Our priorities as a nation are all mixed up. We've lost the direction of common sense. For example, does it make any sense that you can't buy a drink until you are twenty-one, but you can get a firearm when you are eighteen and your brain is still developing? When you're eighteen, you don't know shit and understand even less. The shooter in the Parkland massacre was nineteen. He purchased an AR-15 rifle with multiple clips containing hundreds of rounds. He fired, according to reports, over 150 rounds in just seconds. He purchased all these legally. He killed seventeen (fourteen of them children) and wounded fifteen. In war, that would be considered a serious casualty count.

On the radio talk shows and the TV, you hear again and again how our country stands for this and for that. Same propaganda as usual. But who are these governments and institutions killing their own? Or those who finally can't take it anymore and so they pick up a gun, a brick, or a stone and take it out on innocents? Who are those behind the shadows, the ones actually responsible for these horrible acts of violence? I want to know. We all need to know.

We need to look deeper. For example, has it ever occurred to anyone that maybe our schools are doing something wrong? We need to find the real cause. Was it a broken home, such as in divorce? No family? Rejection? Persecution? Bullied? Pressure? Stress? Or was it simply the neglected outcry for help and attention? Every one of those school shooters suffered at least one or a combination of these dire situations. They are now reacting with rage.

If the stroke of a pen can raise our taxes or start a war, then I'm certain we can do something to protect our children. It's not rocket science philosophy. It's common sense. "Oh, but the Second Amendment says ..." Shut up! The Second Amendment guarantees a constitutional right to bear arms, yes, but it does not preclude reasonable regulation of the most destructive weapons, according to the Supreme Court's *Heller* decision, written by the late conservative Justice Antonin Scalia. Furthermore, the Constitution is not absolute. That's why it has amendments. An amendment, according to *Webster's Dictionary*, is "1. a change for the better; improvement. 2. a correction of errors, faults, etc. 3. a) a revision or addition proposed or made in a bill, law, constitution, etc. b) the process of making such changes." Times have changed; the world has changed. Maybe our Constitution needs to change. Is this so hard to understand?

We, the people, are responsible. The perpetrator is merely a product of failed social and political systems. There are lives in the balance. There are people under fire. Our children are being massacred!

"Be sober, be vigilant; because your adversary the devil walks about like a roaring lion, seeking whom he may devour."
—1 Peter 5:8 NKJV

I repeat: tolerance and complacency are our deadliest enemies.
—(aah)

CHAPTER 24

The Guns

A Reiteration of a National Crisis

As we continue to struggle with the issue of gun control due to the mass shootings in our country, there are some specific steps that can be taken to minimize this tragic and painful problem. And although I have previously talked about school shootings, this is a separate issue in that it involves all mass shootings. So rather than just presenting possible solutions to this problem, I will also present precise and brief justifications for my proposals. These are mostly common sense and practical solutions, things that can be done now.

1. Ban the sale of all assault rifles, AR-15s, and so on.

Make it a federal law. There is no need for this type of weapon in any household. This is a military war weapon, designed to kill foreign enemies and in large volumes and speed. Access to these kinds of weapons makes it easy for those plotting to kill large numbers of innocent people. By banning assault rifles, you can reduce the casualty count by over 50 percent (my personal estimation).

2. Must be twenty-one or older to buy any type of weapon.

If we can set the legal age of twenty-one to drink alcohol, we can certainly do it for the purchase of firearms. A firearm, whether a pistol or a rifle, is much more dangerous and deadlier than an alcoholic beverage. Raising the age limit will make it more difficult for an eighteen-year-old to buy a gun. A twenty-one-year-old is much more mature than an eighteen- or nineteen-year-old. This is common sense.

3. Extensive background checks to include a mental health exam by a registered psychiatrist or psychologist.

Because it has been determined that mental health is a key factor in all of these shootings, it is imperative that every person wanting to own a weapon must be cleared mentally. A psychologically challenged person is not fit to own any type of gun. People with serious mental health problems are dangerous to society. They are unable to think rationally. They see the world the way they want to see it. They judge according to how they feel. They kill without conscience. This requirement is crucial to the process of gun control. Furthermore, it would be a deterrent to anyone wanting to purchase a weapon because of exposure of their mental health condition. Most people do not want their mental health status revealed. It is a clear sign that such a person should not be allowed a weapon. This one is crucial.

4. Offer an incentive for people owning automatic weapons to surrender these weapons by offering them a reasonable monetary amount per weapon.

This proposal would make it possible to remove assault weapons that are out there. There are too many guns in the homes of law-abiding citizens that can easily fall in the wrong hands. Many will take advantage of this incentive because of economic reasons. The surrender of these weapons can be the difference in saving many lives. While some may suggest this is a costly objective, we must never put a price on innocent human life. Get the guns that are out there; they don't need them.

5. Provide federal funding to all public schools for adequate security measures.

Our schools need protection from professional security personnel. These people must be properly trained and fully equipped. They should be strictly assigned to the school. The ideology of arming teachers is reckless. Teachers are to teach. They do not need the burden and liability of carrying firearms. They are already overwhelmed. If we can fund security expenses for federal installations and other entities, we should be able to make our public schools a priority for security measures. I'm certain those in Washington can agree on investing in the safety of our schools. If we can spend billions on other projects, we should be able to protect our children.

Summation: Given the current state of events and political turmoil in our country, it is highly imperative that our representatives know and understand the true sentiments of the people concerning these tragedies that are occurring in our country. From an international terrorist to a simple teenager, our country is under attack. The shootings are brutal. The intent is to kill, and to kill as many as possible. We need answers. We need to find a solution to this madness. We cannot continue like this. Maybe we need to return to our core values that made this country the greatest in the history of humankind. Maybe we need divine intervention. Everything else is failing.

"If My people who are called by My name will
humble themselves, and pray and
seek My face, and turn from their wicked ways, then I will hear
from heaven, and will forgive their sin and
heal their land."
—2 Chronicles 7:14 NKJV

There is a voice out there crying out; the signs are clear.
Are we listening? Are we watching?
—(aah)

CHAPTER 25

We Are Better Than This!

A Philosophical Uplift for Americans

Here's a message of encouragement and edification. It is especially for you. You are the most important person in your life. So here it goes.

Should we wear our most expensive clothing to a ghetto? Why then do we continue to place ourselves in situations that ruin our peace, health, and self-value?

Should we leave our most valuable possessions unguarded in public places? Why then do we place our minds and bodies in the reach of those persons and situations with a demonstrated history of abuse or neglect? We are, to ourselves, the most valuable possession we have. Yet we too often waste our time, energy, and sometimes even our lives in worthless situations among people who are for the most part unworthy or simply unappreciative. We must learn to value our ideas, our energy, our time, and our lives to such an infinite degree that we become unwilling to waste who and what we are. For if we put on our best and go to a mud fight, we can expect to get dirty. If we place our head in the lion's mouth, we should expect to be eaten. Is that what we want? I don't. Do you?

Contrary to traditional beliefs, we were not placed in this world to be poor or to suffer. But we have fallen into the pit of guilt and deceit.

We've allowed ourselves to be caught up in the ways of the world and the philosophies of fools. We do certain things simply because someone tells us to, even though we intuitively know these things are not good for us, nor do we really want to do them. We suffer and struggle in life mostly because we choose to. We strive to please others but too often at a high price. Is it a sin to work hard and enjoy the fruits of our labor, or do we have a lowly and poor God? A professed Christian once said to me of his run-down 1980 Chevette, "That's God's car." He was criticizing my brand-new Pontiac 2000 Ram Air Trans Am, so I replied, "I didn't know God was that poor." He hardly spoke to me after that.

Why do we succumb to inferiorities and meaningless things? The Lord said, "Let the dead bury their dead," yet many live as if they are already dying. Aren't we better than all this?

Who says we are better than no one? Are we not better than filth, ignorance, and stupidity? Or should we conform to the standards of fools? Never! We were created with a price, redeemed with the blood of the Christ. We are too great to be with dogs and too rich to cast our pearls to pigs. We are better than this!

> "Give not which is holy to dogs. Neither cast
> ye your pearls before swine."
> —Matthew 7:6 NKJV

> Trying to please everyone is the surest way to fail.
> —(aah)

CHAPTER 26

The Twelve Signs of a Dictatorship

A Warning to All of Us

Here's a different subject that may be of interest, if not amusing. Though somewhat unlikely, it's a frightening possibility. Read it with an open mind, or whatever mind you may have.

First, I want to define what a dictator is. Basically, "it is a ruler with absolute power and authority, especially one who exercises it tyrannically; a person who orders others about domineeringly, or one whose pronouncements on some subject are meant to be taken as the final word" (*Webster's New World Dictionary*).

There are twelve specific signs that indicate the making of a dictator. These are real and can happen in our country. Here they are:

(1) He puts his name on buildings.
(2) He appoints his family members in positions of power.
(3) His rallies are scary and violent. People get hurt.
(4) He hates the press and criticizes and threatens reporters.
(5) He wants parades and talks a lot about building the military.

(6) He praises other dictators and trash-talks the nations.

(7) He uses the office for personal gain.

(8) He lies so freely people can't tell the difference between truth and lies anymore.

(9) He needs constant flattery from those who support him.

(10) He brags all the time; self-aggrandizement is his greatest pleasure.

(11) He promises the poor everything, then takes away their rights.

(12) He hires and fires at will, getting rid of those who don't agree with him.

Sound familiar? Dictatorships are formed when the people feel suppressed, when they are desperate, when they are most vulnerable. They will listen to lies, even when they know they are lies. When these factors are met, the predator is ready to devour. That's what a dictator really is, a predator. He feeds off the people's woes and their weaknesses. Dictatorships are subtle and insidious movements; you don't see them coming until it's too late. People say nothing like that can happen in America because of our governmental and political structure. Really? Our government is dysfunctional. Many of our politicians claim it is broken. When a government does not work, when there is chaos in it, when there is infighting and dissention within it, it is ripe for a takeover. It is ready for the kill. There are movements right now by different organizations to overthrow our government. The allegation that Russia meddled in the 2016 presidential election is clear evidence that our country is under attack and in danger of becoming a dictatorship. No one really knows the details, but the signs are crystal clear. Those who still believe this cannot happen are those who did not believe the current president could be elected, that he didn't have a chance. We all know differently now, don't we? No, I'm not suggesting that our president is a dictator. But! I'm concerned about the signs I've just presented.

Hitler, Mussolini, Khrushchev—remember those? These men were insidious rulers. They were evil. No one really saw them coming. These kinds of dictators are cunning, sharp, and convincing. They know what they're doing. There are still many like them today, including in our country, the United States of America. The only reason they haven't been able to take over is because the people are not desperate enough. Whatever the case may be, whatever lies we may be told, all we have to do is follow the twelve signs of a dictatorship!

And all who dwell on the earth will worship him, whose names have not
been written in the Book of Life of the Lamb slain from the
foundation of the world.
—Revelation 13:8 NKJV

You don't see them coming …
—(aah)

CHAPTER 27

A Veteran's Plea

A Letter to the President

Although this letter is from a veteran (me), it represents similar struggles of many Americans whose benefits and entitlements are under fire. It is a problem that could drastically affect the entire American economy.

> Dear President Trump:
>
> I am a disabled Vietnam war veteran. It has come to my attention that there is a provision in your budget plan that contains a proposal that would scale back VA's Individual Unemployability (IU) program for thousands of American veterans.
>
> Be advised that the IU program was designed into law for veterans who are determined to be unemployable as a result of service-connected disabilities resulting at the 100 percent rate. It is for veterans who have serious medical problems and who cannot work, and for their families, to pay for essentials such as food, transportation, rent, a mortgage, and utilities, all of which have risen in

costs. Our water, electricity, and gas fees have increased considerably. Each year it gets harder to pay these expenses on fixed and limited incomes.

The elimination of IU compensation for disabled veterans will cause great and undue hardship on all veterans in receipt of IU and their families. It would not only affect the veterans' family income, but other critical ancillary benefits, such as Dental Coverage, Survivors' and Dependents' Educational Assistance, the Civilian Health and Medical Program of the VA (CHAMPVA), commissary and exchange privileges, and the value of Social Security benefits. Additionally, this would impact access to some state benefits such as property tax exemptions for veteran homeowners, free vehicle registration and free access to state parks (parks are good therapy for veterans with PTSD). These are crucial for a veterans' livelihood and for an acceptable quality of life.

Another area that would be impacted is the economy. If veterans do not have money to spend, that struggling waitress with a family at our favorite restaurant will not see a generous gratuity anymore. That car dealer where we get our vehicles from will go out of business. Organizations dependant on donations too will feel the impact. These are just a few examples of how the economy would be affected.

As veterans, we are already strained in obtaining the medical care we need. We don't need to worry about paying our bills. We have enough problems in life. Our days are numbered. Many of us are simply suffering. When you're rated as disabled and unemployable, that means you have a serious medical condition or conditions; you are not having fun.

Balancing budgets on the backs of veterans is not right. It will only hurt those who depend on their pensions to survive. A veterans' pension is his/her livelihood. For most, it's the only income they have. In fact, most veterans are living well below the poverty level. Reducing or taking away our benefits is morally wrong and unwise. It is vehemently unacceptable.

As a Vietnam war veteran who has seen and buried the dead, I often wonder, what did we go to war for? What did we fight for? Did we do it so that someday we'll debate about who can go to what bathroom? Did we do it so that politicians could sign bills that would spin us into poverty? Did we do it so that someday the government would betray us and take away the benefits we've earned? NO! We went to war for our country at a time when it was not a popular thing to do, when we didn't have a choice. We've paid our dues.

Our wives have seen our anger and tears. They've heard our screams at night because of the constant nightmares of war. They've witnessed our addiction to drugs given to us by the VA for our ailments (a huge problem in the VA right now). They've taken us to the emergency room and to our VA appointments more times than most of us care to admit. And now, our government wants to take away our "benefits?" Those who have not served in the military do not realize the boundaries they should not cross. Cutting veterans' benefits is a dangerous boundary to cross, Mr. President.

As veterans, we are the backbone of this country, not the politicians, not our institutions, not our banks, not the courts, not even our churches, but those men who know what the price for freedom is. I speak not only for myself, but for all veterans and their families, and especially for those who shed their blood for the freedoms that you, yourself, enjoy. Yes, Mr. President, we deserve much better than this.

Furthermore, I must alert you. Cutting veterans' benefits could result in very serious ramifications such as rampant bankruptcies, increased homelessness, massive suicides, and violent protests, problems our country doesn't need right now. The shooting of June 14 in

Alexandria, VA, in which a congressman, his aide, and two officers were shot, is a clear example of what can happen when someone gets angry enough. They were shot by an American citizen who was fed up with the politics of the times. According to CNN reports, he specifically targeted politicians. One senator said it was a wake-up call to all politicians. I mention this, Mr. President, because I myself have overheard the hostile chatter between veterans at the VA where I go for my appointments. I don't like what I hear, some of it is very disturbing. Also, the tragedy that occurred at the VA clinic here in El Paso in January of 2015, in which a veteran and ex-VA employee shot and killed a VA psychiatrist, then himself, shocked everyone. People thought that something like that could never happen at this VA, but it did. To this day, many have not gotten over it. In fact, many have left. My own VA doctor resigned the very next day, after the incident. Hundreds of patients were affected. This is what everyone should know, what "you" should know. That Afghanistan war veteran who shot and killed three staff members at a California VA treatment center for PTSD veterans did it because he was denied care. He sought care but no one listened. The result, an administrator and two clinicians lost their lives that day. That VA facility will never be the same. Cutting, reducing, taking away veteran's benefits will cause havoc in this country. This is not an opinion, it is a fact.

One more thing, Mr. President, we also … VOTE! Yes, veterans vote. We are very astute as to who to vote for and why. Many veterans voted for you. We voted for you because you assured us of our rights and benefits as veterans. You vowed to improve the VA health care system, a system that is in "critical condition." You appointed a new VA secretary to straighten out the VA. You promised us we would lack nothing. We trusted you. Now, we face losing a critical benefit and right that was awarded to us for our service to our country.

America owes an apology to every veteran who went to war for this country, and who now faces the possibility of having his/her benefits stripped. Is this how our country repays our veterans? Please, Mr. President, reconsider. Cutting or taking away veterans' benefits is NOT the way to 'Make America Great Again.'

Very Respectfully,
Albert A. Hernandez

That was my letter to the president. He has vowed to answer our letters and our emails. And he did. That is why it is highly imperative that we, as veterans, take a stand and speak up for what we've earned, not only for ourselves but for our families and all Americans who have earned what is theirs and for their families. What we do or don't do today will determine the fate of our children and grandchildren. We're Americans. An American fights for what's right, for what's theirs. Or did those who died for our freedom and rights die in vain? My God, I hope not! Consider the following:

> With malice toward none, with charity for all, with firmness
> in the right as God gives us to see the right, let us strive on to
> finish the work we are in, to bind up the nation's wounds, to
> care for him who shall have borne the battle and for his widow,
> and his orphan, to do all which may achieve and cherish a just
> and lasting peace among ourselves and with all nations.
> —Abraham Lincoln

> "But if anyone does not provide for his own,
> and especially for those of his
> household, he has denied the faith and is worse than an unbeliever."
> —1 Timothy 5:8 NKJV

> What makes us the greatest country in the world is the manner in
> which we take care of our own.
> —(aah)

Chapter 28

When I Was a Kid

A Sentimental Memoir

When I was a kid, we didn't have a lot. We had one TV, black and white. One car. My dad did not believe in an allowance. If we wanted money, we had to work for it. I earned mine by cutting lawns on Saturdays, working a paper route, and selling doughnuts after school. On a good week, I would make about twelve dollars. In those days, that was a lot of money for a kid.

When I was a kid, I had a bike, a BB gun, and a baseball glove, and I built models. I played cowboys and Indians with my friends. I played Little League baseball and sandlot football. Once I even thought I was Johnny Unitas. Remember him? I could throw a football about forty yards at the age of twelve. I could throw a softball almost a hundred yards. I was good at whatever I did.

When I was a kid, we settled our differences with a good-ole fistfight. The school bully was no more than another kid who thought he was tougher than everyone else. Hit him once, and he even became your best friend.

When I was a kid, we ate together at the dinner table. We had to wait until Dad got home before we ate. Mom did not have to work. She took care of the home. Dad was in the air force. We lived in Maine, Georgia, New York, and Louisiana. Each one was an adventure.

When I was a kid, parents and teachers ruled. When Dad said no, he meant no. When your teacher gave you a command, you did it. Obedience and respect were not an option.

When I was a kid, there were no mass shootings in our schools; no drugs. We would say the Pledge of Allegiance, and through the intercom, someone led us in the Lord's Prayer. That's how we started the school day. God protected us from evil.

When I was a kid, we didn't have computers, cell phones, or calculators. Just brains and the discipline to learn. English, math, science, history, and physical education were all we needed.

When I was a kid, you addressed your elders with "Yes, sir" and "Yes, ma'am." Your dad was not the old man. He was your father. Your mother was not the old lady. She was your mother.

When I was a kid, we didn't notice whether we were white or black. Race and color meant nothing to us, just friendship. Abortion and homosexuality were unheard of.

When I was a kid, things were simpler and better. Anger and hate were just words. Today, these kill.

When I was a kid, going to church was a very sacred thing. We listened to the priest or pastor in fear. We knew right from wrong. Fear of the Lord was instilled in us.

Dear God, what happened to those days when ... I was a kid?

"Assuredly, I say to you, unless you are converted and become as little children, you will by no means enter the kingdom of heaven."
—Matthew 18:3 NKJV

We can still be kids if we really try.
—(aah)

Chapter 29

Being a True American

It is disgracefully unfair that, compared to the overall population of the United States of America, only a small fraction of it serve in the military, and fewer go to war for it. There is something very wrong with this equation.

An American is not a full-fledge American until he has served his country in a military uniform. This may sound rather radical, but it's true. It is grossly unfair that today's soldiers are called to war more than their share while millions at home sit back and enjoy the comfort of the freedoms these guys are fighting for in the frontlines. Again, something is very wrong here.

You see, it is easy to be patriotic, until you've felt the sting of battle. It is easy to fly the flag, proclaiming to be a proud American, until you've seen your combat buddy full of holes from the bullets that ripped through his body or a land mine that tore his body to shreds. Yes, it's easy to be a civilian and say, "I'm proud to be an American." Are you really?

There is no comparison between civilians and the military. Being born in this country, working hard, raising a family, and paying taxes are not enough to call yourself a true American, I dare say. It's like the faithful churchgoer who says, "I'm a Christian," but who has never lifted a finger to serve in the church or sacrificed anything in the ministry of the Lord.

They are religious hypocrites. Like some of those preachers who talk the good talk and preach a great sermon, as if they are so holy and righteous, when in fact they are sometimes worse sinners than the flock and haven't a clue what it means to be a soldier, a marine, a sailor, or an airman. These are the ones who really make my blood boil!

Remember the draft? Every male born in this country, regardless of status or race, should be called to service in the military at the age of eighteen or until he finishes high school. No exceptions, unless he is specifically proven to be physically or mentally unfit. The same should apply to male immigrants coming to this country legally. They should have to serve in our military if they desire to stay here and become citizens. In fact, service in our military should be a prerequisite to becoming an American citizen. Let me clear up the immigration problem while I'm at it: After a maximum of at least six years, if an immigrant is not an American citizen, they go back to their native country. Remember, these are civilians from another country wanting to come into our country to reap the benefits of American citizenship. That's okay, but they must earn it; they must suffer for it. Now, as for our women, the military should be an option but under strict military law and regulations, and none of this women's rights crap. The military was designed to fight wars, not to bear children. The military should never be used as a welfare system of benefits.

Speaking of benefits, anyone who believes that military benefits are too generous should visit their local recruiting office and sign up. A career in the military will change their way of thinking and make them appreciate the benefits of being a true American, instead of increasing the burden on those who have served in their place. We as Americans—that is, those who have served and who are now serving in the military—should be outraged at the inequity concerning citizenship and service to our country. It's not right for a twenty-year-old to be sitting at home, doing drugs, defaming the flag, and mocking our country while there are those in faraway countries fighting dangerous and dirty wars. My blood boils when I think of this. It has to. I buried too many guys in Vietnam.

Today, we're in a hell of a spiritual war for the very soul and fate of this country. I say "hell" because that's what we're dealing with. We are seeing it in our government, a dysfunctional and corrupt government that cares more about the immigrant than the rights of its citizens. The last government shutdown over immigrants proved this. And it's not over yet. Our rights as Americans are seriously being challenged. Our core values that made this country the greatest and mightiest are being erased by our very own institutions. That recent same-sex marriage between two gay army helicopter pilots at West Point made me sick … literally. That is not the America I know and was raised in. But that's where we're at. So when I have the opportunity to express my views and convictions and to help where ever I can, I will. I will not keep silent. My words have power, because they are truth!

Our country was formed through men who believed in God. It was given to us with the beautiful and sacred ideology of freedom. Too much American blood has been shed over it, and I don't want to lose it over some stupid, politically correct nonsense.

As an American citizen and a war veteran, I know what it means to be an American. I know what it means to love my country. I expect no less from anyone else and apologize to no one for my country. May God bless the United States of America!

> "I declare today to the Lord your God that I
> have come to the country which
> the Lord swore to our fathers to give us."
> —Deuteronomy 26:3 NKJV

> Our country is only as great as our people are.
> —(aah)

CHAPTER 30

A Conversation with God

H ave you ever talked to God? I mean, really talked to God? I have. The following is a hypothetical conversation of mine with God. It is something I have thought about and dreamed about over and over. It's a spiritual conviction that does not let me rest. It is based on facts and the truth of God. It is a testimonial of my faith in God. There is nothing wrong with talking to God, I have found. For the person who seeks God will find God. God will reveal Himself in many ways, some very scary. This writing of mine is evidence of that, for who would dare to write such words? How does someone come up with these things? He doesn't. It's what the Spirit reveals to him. Nevertheless, here it is. Read it with an open mind and between the lines. There is a spiritual imperative here.

Albert: Dear Lord, a while back, I talked to You about an event that took place at the White House. It was on a Sunday, November 14, 2010, on *60 Minutes*, where the Medal of Honor was awarded to a soldier by the president. That was good. But then they showed how the war in Afghanistan was going. That was not good. Since then, many things have transpired in our country, such as mass shootings in our schools, bombings, terrorists' threats, and the incident that happened in our local VA in January where a doctor was shot and killed by an ex-VA employee.

That really hit home. There has been much talk about how bad our country is doing and that it is deteriorating into total ruin. Preachers are preaching we are in the end-times. Is this true? I'm asking You because I'm very worried about the way things are going; like the elections, the wars, drugs, health care, the jobless, the homeless, the economy, same-sex marriages, homosexuality, and so on. Many are now calling us a "fading republic," including some Americans themselves. In fact, there is a book written with that title. Can You please give me Your perspective on this? I'm worried about my country. I'm worried about many things.

God: Good points. But you may not like My comments. I have some very strong things to say about America. Are you sure you want to hear them?

Albert: Yes, go ahead. I'm ready. I need to know. I'm an American and a war veteran. I'm really concerned. I love my country.

God: Yes, I know you do. You served your country and ministry faithfully and honorably. I am proud of you. But it has been a long time since your government and its institutions openly admitted that you needed God to have this nation work properly. Nowadays, people either ignore Me or are openly hostile to Me. Symbols that remind you of Me are not allowed in most public places. TV and Hollywood name Me frequently but usually in a blasphemous manner, and too many of you fall for this. Your government prohibits prayer in many areas. Students may not mention My name in the classroom, yet no one can stop them when it is used in vain in the hallways or school grounds. Same is the case in government facilities and institutions. You can say the GD word, but you don't dare say "Jesus Christ" because you might offend someone and you'll get reported, maybe even sued. Am I right?

Albert: Yes, very. I hear it on the national news quite often. I hear how many churches are allowing same-sex marriages, something that makes me sick.

God: Yes, I know how you feel. However, it is not unusual for a nation to ignore Me. The story of nations is a story of unbelief and the lack of fear of God. Usually, as a nation prospers, the people ignore or forget Me. Then, as it falls on hard times, they seek Me but often too late. That severe weather you are experiencing is not Mother Nature. It is Me. I am in control. I am God! I control the weather. I determine your every breath.

You ignore Me and My commandments at your own peril. Families, institutions, and whole cultures crumble when I am ignored. History has shown you this over and over, and your country, the United States of America, as great as it is, is never exempt from My judgment. America is now to the point where it is rapidly deteriorating into physical and spiritual death. Your growing and complex problems of crime, drug abuse, divorce, teenage pregnancy, homosexuality, disease, abortion, child abuse, homelessness, violence, education, and of course war are all rooted in your choice to ignore Me and My will. These are now taking a heavy toll on your country. For example, what has happened in Mexico can easily happen in America too. For years, they have worshipped their version of God by praying to idols and all those religious figurines fabricated by their religion. They've become irresponsible by having children they can't support, and their government has become increasingly corrupt. Evil has plagued that entire country. That's why thousands are fleeing to your country, causing the immigration problem. That's why I am not listening to their prayers. America is heading in that same direction. You are becoming apostates. You have deviated from My laws. Am I getting through to you?

Albert: Yes, I'm afraid so (literally afraid).

God : That's good. I'm glad someone is listening. Your government, for example, has become a farce, and there are serious problems in all areas of leadership. Your previous president, who was alleged by many to be a Muslim, was elected with the desperate hope that he would bring about change. Well, you got it. Yet you are still plagued with the same problems, only worse. Your new president is causing havoc. Many consider him a worse president and a danger. Your enemies are laughing at him. Speaking of enemies, your enemy is not the Iranians, the Russians, the North Koreans, Al Qaeda, ISIS, and all those others you consider enemies. Your enemy is yourselves. Just look at the VA, for example, the place where you worked and get your health care. It's a mess. You had to retire because it made you sick, and now they're telling you all the time that it's worse. When you were there, you were the minister. You were a powerful testimonial to My ways. But when you left, they felt your absence. Bad things started to happen, and the following year, your organization was rated worst in the nation. It made the headlines. The "worst in the nation" rap that your VA got was actually a warning sign. But still they didn't listen. So their next judgment became more severe. Why? Because a man of God spoke out but was ostracized and ignored. That man was you, My son. And remember, I deal with your enemies, not you. Leave the judgment to Me.

Albert: Oh, Lord, I didn't look at it that way. But I still don't quite understand what you mean that that the enemy is ourselves. That really bothers me.

God: Well, it should. Consider the caliber of your past and present administration. It has been clear evidence that ethics and integrity mean very little these days, much less biblical principles. The one candidate who professed Me in the campaign of 2004 was ignored and mocked; he didn't have a chance. This was because the main interest at the time was your economy. That is, the majority were selling out to what they thought was the American dream. Instead, right now, many of you are experiencing an uncertain job market and a disturbing increase of destitute people. Your unemployment rate is still too high. Job security and freedom are an illusion, and many of you are terrified at the mere thought of losing your jobs or your pensions. Just about every day you hear that things are getting worse. How about those violent protests over black men killed by white cops in your major cities? It's on the national news all the time. Someone is getting killed almost every day by the very ones who are supposed to serve and protect. Want me to continue?

Albert: Yes, I might as well get it all now. I mean, I see the signs, and I've studied the scriptures. They're frightening.

God : Good! They should be. You're not as blind as many others are. Remember, you're a studied minister; you know these things. I did not spare you from war for nothing. But I'll tell you anyway. In effect, you are already experiencing biblical prophecies and warning signs. Still, there is no real repentance or change in American lifestyles. Pleasure, greed, and power are the themes of the times. I, the Creator of everything you see, have been treated as though I am nothing more than just a member of the religious mob. My Word is mocked, and My truth is ignored by many. But it is I who'll have the last word. It is I who am going to bring strict judgment on those who continue in their sinful ways. "Every knee will bow ..." and every knee will. As a nation that has seriously deviated from the Godly principles it was founded upon, I will destroy America if it continues like that. All the bad things that have happened to your country in the past forty years are not mere coincidences or bad luck. The 9/11 attack was not just an attack by an enemy that hates you. All of these things happened for a much higher reason and purpose. It taught you that you are not indivisible. You could have averted that attack, but I allowed it to happen to get your attention. Remember how patriotic and religious you all got? Remember the fear? Have I gotten your attention?

Albert: Oh, yes. I hate the way things are right now, like the stupid security measures at the airports and now at our local VA. People are treated like suspects. I call it paranoia.

God: Call it what you want, but understand what's really going on. It is unwise to ignore Me. There are now specific signs that the end is near and that I am growing tired of a nation that continues in its blatant sin and simply is not listening to Me. Remember Sodom and Gomorra? You are becoming more and more like them. In many cases, even your churches are not listening, as they too are doing their own thing. You have women preachers ordained as ministers, homosexuals as pastors, and corrupt and immoral priests. Church pastors are demanding more and more from their flocks while they enjoy their expensive cars and luxurious homes. These are not My ways! Yet the majority of you seem to approve of these things. You are so dependent on a government that is considered broken and dysfunctional. Your laws are practically worthless. Your schools are dangerously out of control, and your churches are weak. Are you sure you want Me to continue?

Albert: Yes. (He saw my tears. I didn't expect these kinds of responses. I felt like I was being lectured to.)

God: Okay, here's another huge problem that's seriously plaguing your country. It's one I want you to preach about the next sermon you give. When the head of the household (the man) fails to take charge, when the woman of the household (the wife) refuses to subject to her husband, and when the children refuse to obey their parents, the family crumbles. There is divorce. "God hates divorce." The man and wife go their separate ways, and the children are lost. The same thing happens with a country. There is dissention, and it eventually crumbles. When the family falls apart, the country falls apart, no matter how strong it is, militarily or politically. It's that simple. I am telling you this because the divorce rate in the United States of America is now estimated at 80 percent according to your numbers. But My numbers are much higher, and this does not include the increasing domestic violence that you hear about a lot on the local news nowadays. You're more concerned about your economy than the sanctity of marriage and family. This sin alone is destroying your country. Look at your local city government. Your city council wants to revoke your vote on the issue about granting equal health benefits to unmarried and gay partners. The majority voted no, but now they want to repeal it because it's politically incorrect. Your political correctness is killing you, and your votes mean very little these days. You wrote a letter to the editor about this, and it was rejected. Why? Because they don't want to hear the truth, My truth!

Albert: I voted, but I didn't think it would get that serious.

God: Well, it is, and here's more. Pay attention. Have you witnessed the increasing tragedies and natural disasters lately? People are dying at an alarming rate everywhere. You're feeling sorry for those countries that are suffering earthquakes, severe weather, famine, disease, and everything else that is killing them. But those are countries that have rejected My Word and practice witchcraft, voodoo, sorcery, and other evil things. Yet, in your country, people are losing their homes, their dreams, everything. Things they've worked for all their lives are suddenly gone. You are not winning your wars, and the price you are paying for these wars is much too high. Again, these are not just coincidences or bad luck. No, these are warning signs with a divine purpose. You don't need a lot of theology here to grasp this. You don't need Christian counselors to explain your sin. You don't need your psychologists or psychiatrists telling you why your people are killing each other and committing suicide. And you certainly don't need those vociferous fools from the pulpits telling you what to do, and then they want your money too. No, you don't need all these things. What you need is Me in your lives. You need Me in your homes, your schools, in the workplace, and, yes, in your churches too! Until then, no matter what you do and no matter who your leaders are, Democrat or Republican, black or white, or whatever you call yourselves, it is meaningless and hopeless. Are you getting all this?

Albert: Crystal clear, Lord. Crystal clear!

God: Some will object to this message and say that America is still the greatest country. Yes, so once was the Roman Empire. So once was the English Empire. So once was the French Empire. Remember your history? Remember what happened to them? All fell in a very short time. One of them fell in just one day! Think about that. As a country, you no longer have the luxury of turning the other way and ignoring Me. The time has come for you to start taking a serious look at yourselves and quit blaming the other nations for your sin. They will receive their just reward. You just follow and obey Me. Your political slogan, "God bless America," means nothing to Me. It's what you do that will matter in the end. Enough?

Albert: Whew! Yes. But I have one more question, and I fear asking it. About twelve years ago, I was doing great. Why did you allow certain illnesses to inflict me? Aren't You the Great Healer? And why am I still tormented about Vietnam? That was many years ago. Why? Why, Lord?

God: Yes, I am the Great Healer. But that was twelve years ago. And remember, when you are weak, I am stronger. So don't think about your ailments. You're being taken care of. Focus more on the blessings I have bestowed upon you. As for Vietnam, that's an experience you had to go through to make you the person you are today. You did some very good things over there. Be proud of that. It wasn't all combat. Remember that little Vietnamese infant you rendered care to, the one you sent a picture of to your *Veterans' Voices* magazine? I loved the writeup they did about you. Remember that boy that was shot down from a tree and they called on you to treat his wounds? I saw all that. And don't forget, I saved you from that terrible war. I don't want you to forget about that experience, because if you do, you are of no use to anyone. Understanding and compassion are your strongest traits, your ministry. Remember this too: you're getting well compensated for it. You're better off than most. I, your God, made sure of that and will continue to do so. In your darkest moments, I was there with you. And I have chastised your enemies. My angels are always with you. Don't forget that.

Albert: Wow! Thank you, my Lord. Now, what do you want me to do? I mean, is there anything else I can do? Sometimes I feel inadequate. Sometimes I just don't feel good. Sometimes I …

God: Quit your whining. You've done your part. You've saved the souls that needed to be saved. Now just enjoy your life. You have a great wife, a nice home, and you're not poor. You have a great gift. Now use it. Continue to do what you've always done. Be yourself. Pray for those who need prayer. Fight the good fight. Stay clean from the world. Avoid those who are evil-minded. You know who they are. I'll deal with them. Now, quote me your favorite verse in the Bible, the one you try very hard to live by. I like that one Myself.

Albert: Really? You do? How do you know which one? (Dumb question.)

God: I know the number of hairs on your head. I know how many you lost this morning when you showered. I knew your questions before you even asked them. I knew you before you were born.

Albert: Oops. Here it is: "For God did not give us a spirit of timidity, but a spirit of power, love and self-discipline" (1 Timothy 1:7).

God: Very good! Now take your medication and go to bed.

Albert: Can I share this conversation with others?

God: Of course you can. I'm open to anyone who truly seeks Me. Now go to bed! Oh, one more thing, my son: this conversation was *not* hypothetical!

A chill went through me. Speaking to God can be scary. Be careful what you ask. Prepare yourself for the answers. You may not like some of them.

> The fear of the Lord is the beginning of wisdom, and
> knowledge of the Holy One is understanding.
> —Proverbs 9:10 NKJV

> Speaking to God is a scary thing but also very wise.
> —(aah)

CHAPTER 31

Revolution!

Taking Back Our Nation

The truth is we need a revolution! We need a revolution to take back our nation, to turn our nation and its people back to the core values that made this country the greatest in the world.

"Revolution" is defined in *Webster's Dictionary* as "a sudden and dramatic change." Our country has been in need of a dramatic change for many years. We need a revolution, a real revolution, a revolution that will change our country, the world, and each and every one of us, you and me!

But why? Why a sudden change? Why a revolution? Here's why: when our schools are directing our children to use the bathroom they need to use, according to the gender with which they now identify as transgenders and gays; when two gay army helicopter pilots are allowed to marry each other at West Point; when the US Air Force Academy allows a pagan worship service and a Marine Corps officer is court-martialed and thrown out of the military for having a Bible verse in her computer system (these were reported on a CNN program several years ago, as I recall; I wrote these down for further reference); when our churches have abandoned the preaching of God's Word for a watered-down version that teaches no consequence for sinful lifestyles; when our political leaders openly lie to us and want to take away from the poor and give more to the rich; when our policemen blatantly shoot innocent men due to race and color and get away with it; when we continue to send our men and women to wars we don't intend to win, then not care for them when they return, or their widows; when we allow athletes to openly show disrespect to the flag and the national anthem and call it freedom of speech; when our veterans kill themselves because of a health care system that has failed them; when our government cannot balance the budget but can give other countries billions in aid; when those dreamers and immigrants are more important than the rights of bona fide American citizens; when our kids are being massacred in our schools by some angry psychopath due to society's ignorance; and when political correctness takes precedence over God's principles and laws, yes, we need a sudden and dramatic change. We need a revolution!

Whether we know it or not, we went through a revolution in the late 1960s. It was caused by the Vietnam War. There were violent protests going on everywhere in the nation. People were getting hurt and killed. Buildings were set on fire. There was extreme lawlessness. The military could not control the behavior of many of its enlistees as they fled to Mexico and Canada. There was chaos all over. It was ugly. Politically, the government had to give in; it realized the country was in serious trouble. That's how Nixon became president. He promised the nation he would end the Vietnam War and bring back everyone home. So he won the election. We got out of Vietnam in a disgraceful manner. The people back home demanded we get out of there. It was a national revolution that forced the end of that war. That is what really happened.

Our country was formed through a violent revolution. It was called the Revolutionary War of 1775. General George Washington, our first president, led his army against the British Empire. He was outmanned and outgunned, but they were victorious. They were victorious because they believed in God. Washington prayed all the time. We became a nation, a nation under God. It took a revolution for our country to survive and become the mightiest in the world.

It is time for all Americans to stand up to the status quo and boldly and unashamedly speak their mind. I am talking about real Americans, those who truly love this country and believe in the true God and not some flimflam religion that just goes through their rigid motions. The world is full of all that.

We must take this country back, back to what it used to be. Simply put, we need a revolution!

> When the righteous thrive, the people rejoice;
> when the wicked rule, the people
> groan.
> —Proverbs 29:2 NKJV

Whenever any government routinely and continually goes beyond the consent of the governed, free men must resist its tyrannical usurpations, even at the risk of their lives and fortunes, as required by sacred honor.
—Natural Rights and the American Revolution

CHAPTER 32

Christianity

How It Is Different from Every Religion

I have discussed the subject of religion in a previous section. But this is not religion. This is Christianity, the basis of our eternal salvation after this life. Yes, there is an afterlife. So pay attention to what I have to say; this may be the most important section of the book. I am dealing with the soul, not the intellect. Because what we believe, or don't believe, does not change the truth.

Christianity has several major differences from every other religion on earth. If someone asked you, "What is different about Christianity?" what would you say to them?

One big example is the central defining moment of human history—when Jesus Christ rose from the dead after three days. No other god or person has ever done that, nor does any other religion make that same claim.

Another key difference is that the central text of Christianity is the Holy Bible. The Bible is the only ancient document that accurately describes the true nature of human beings. It is the Word of God talking to humankind.

If you were to study other religions, you would note that there is always a checklist of tasks that you must carry out in order to reach paradise. Islam, for example, teaches that your good deeds and bad deeds will be weighed on a scale; you will only reach paradise in that faith if your good deeds outweigh your bad deeds (or if you strap on some dynamite and take the terrorist shortcut). In the religion of global warming, you can be forgiven of your carbon sins by purchasing enough carbon credits from Al Gore. Have you ever listened to this once presidential candidate?

Jehovah's Witnesses, Mormons and many other faiths have salvation checklists. You have to meet their rules in order to achieve salvation. This is basically known as "works salvation," and the philosophy behind this permeates many areas of life. It was embodied by JFK's famous statement, "Ask not what your country can do for you; ask what you can do for your country." Remember that one? It sounds good, but it is not God's Word.

So, what is different about Christianity when compared to all the world's other religions? What do you have to do to achieve salvation in Christianity? I'll make it very simple: Jesus Christ. The term Christianity is derived from His name: *Christ*ianity. Only through Him can we enter the paradise of heaven when we die. Oh, yes, there is a heaven ... and a hell. Where we go depends on what we believe, and the scriptures are very clear:

> "I am the way, the truth, and the life. No one
> comes to the Father except through Me."
> —John 14:6 NKJV

> And we know that the Son of God has come
> and has given us an understanding,
> that we may know Him who is true, in His Son Jesus Christ.
> This is the true God and eternal life.
> —1 John 5:20 NKJV

> When you reject truth, all that's left is a lie.
> —John Hagee

CHAPTER 33

Summation

Oftentimes in our modern world we confuse what makes nations great. We believe that if we've got a good governmental structure then we'll have a great nation, but that's not true, because governments are only as good as the people who run them. Other people, other nations, they believe that a superior military power is what makes a nation great, and while having more men in uniform and more weapons and more resources might be intimidating to your enemies, the reality of it is that no army is any better than the men who wear the uniform. There are a lot of people who believe that if you've got a strong economy and you're financially sound, then you're going to be a great nation, but the reality of it is if you've got all of the wealth of the world but you have a corrupt moral code you'll destroy yourself with your resources. The greatest resource that any nation has is NOT it's government, is NOT it's military, is NOT it's financial strength. The greatest resource that any nation has are godly people who are willing to do godly things, in it. A government will not make America great again. Only the people can do that.

You and I, with the privilege to live in the United States of America, must remember that we are a nation created by the sovereignty and the providence of God. I don't care what lie you've heard lately, the truth is when you look at the foundations of this nation's fabric, God's fingerprints are all over it. His grace is what birthed our Republic. His sovereign power is the source from where we draw our liberty. The words of His truth are the principles from which we molded our Constitution, from where we poured our freedoms … He has chosen the United States.

The Bible says, "Righteousness exalts a nation, but sin is a reproach to many people." We are under the spell of political correctness. We live in a world where a humanist agenda doesn't tolerate disagreement. If you have a different opinion than what they have, they'll sue you, they'll speak out against you. If you stand up they'll subpoena you. If you press forward they'll throw you into court. They'll destroy you if you disagree. But if you're standing upon the truth, disagree with boldness and make it count.

We have a society … they've exalted the environment to the point that we've taught our children how to protect mother earth but we haven't taught them how to worship Father God. We have a nation like Jezebel's nation, since Roe v. Wade, where we have sacrificed 60 million children on the alter of abortion clinics, all to the god of self.

That was an excerpt of a sermon by pastor Matthew Hagee from Cornerstone Church in San Antonio, Texas, titled "Make it Count." It was a fiery and powerful message, a message to our nation in that we have deviated from the principles of God's laws and that we will perish if we continue in our ways. I fully believe what he said is true. I concur.

The truth is we have become a society of greed and selfishness. We want more but offer less. The doctor wants a larger salary. The hospital wants higher profits. The people demand better and affordable health care but continue to abuse the system and their bodies. The immigrant wants rights and privileges they haven't earned. The soldier is sent to a war he can't win, then is denied rights and benefits he has earned. The professional athlete defies the flag and gets paid millions. The banks want your home. Our political leaders openly lie to us, promising us things they've no intention of delivering. From the highest to the lowest, corruption and greed reign. All this is killing our nation. It is a subtle deception that is destroying the very core values that formed our country. Complacency and tolerance are the two major daggers piercing our hearts and minds. We have been brainwashed. We have been duped by fools.

But wait! There is hope! Where there is truth, there is power. We have the power! You and me! We have the power when we exercise and proclaim the truth. Truth always prevails no matter what. Powerful men have been brought to their knees by truth. But we must be bold and daring, strong and determined. We must proclaim the truth at all times. We must face the truth and use it. We must speak it, write it, and teach it. It's called the audacity of truth.

"For the wrath of God is revealed from heaven against all ungodliness
and unrighteousness of men, who suppress the truth in
unrighteousness."
—Romans 1:18 NKJV

My heart and mind have spoken. My soul is crying out.
I have spoken the truth.
—(aah)

TRUTH: the quality or state of being true; the quality
of being in accordance with experience,
facts, or reality; reality, actual existence; that which is true; statement, etc.
that accords with fact or reality; an established or verified fact,
principle, etc.; a particular belief or teaching regarded
by the speaker as the true one.
—*Webster's New World Dictionary*

The contents of this book have been written in good faith and are not meant to discredit anyone or defame anyone. They are based mostly on the scriptures and the author's knowledge and experience. It is for the edification and salvation of our nation.

—Albert A. Hernandez

BIBLIOGRAPHY

Black, Henry Campbell, MA. *Black's Law Dictionary*. St. Paul, MN: West Publishing Co., 1979.

Blocher, Mark. *Vital Signs*. Printed in the Unites States of America, 1992.

Clark, Margaret, editor in chief. *Veterans Voices Writing Project*. Established as Hospitalized Veterans Writing Project by Elizabeth Fontaine in 1946. Kansas City, MO: Board of Veterans Voices Writing Project, fall 2006 to present.

Fletcher, C., Norman Quist, and Albert R. Jonsen. *Ethics Consultation in Health Care*. Ann Arbor, MI: Health Administration Press, 1989.

Hagee, John C., editor. *Prophecy Study Bible and Ministries*. Scripture taken from the New King James Version, copyright 1979, 1980, 1982, by Thomas Nelson, Inc. Printed in Colombia, 2007. John Hagee Ministries, Cornerstone Church, San Antonio, TX.

Hagee, Matthew. *Shaken, Not Shattered*. Lake Mary, FL: Charisma House, a Strang Company, 2009.

Hernandez, Albert A., DBA. "Critical Issues in American Health Care." Doctoral thesis, Southern California University for Professional Studies, 1997.

Jackson, Monique F., MRA. *Patient Administration and Medical Records*. Personal interview, William Beaumont Army Medical Center, El Paso, TX, 1985.

Koop, C. Everett, MD, and Timothy Johnson, MD. *Let's Talk*. Grand Rapids, MI: Zondervan Publishing House, 1992.

Martin, Walter. *The Kingdom of the Cults*. Minneapolis, MI: Bethany House Publishers, 1985.

Pozgar, George D., MBA. *Legal Aspects of Health Care Administration.* Gaithersburg, MD: Aspen Publishers, Inc., 1993.

Rosten, Leo. *Religions of America.* New York, NY: Simon & Schuster, Inc., 1975.

Southwick, Arthur F. *The Law of Hospital and Health Care Administration.* Ann Arbor, MI: Health Administration Press, 1988.

Tada, Joni Earickson. *When Is It Right to Die?* Grand Rapids, MI: Zondervan Publishing House, 1992.

You did not just happen. You were created from the substance of the Almighty, and because of this fact, you, like all other created things, cannot properly survive or function apart from your foundational source.

—Matthew Hagee

www.ingramcontent.com/pod-product-compliance
Lightning Source LLC
Chambersburg PA
CBHW020517290526
45786CB00002B/638